COLLINS

Gardeners'
CALENDAR

ADAM PASCO

HarperCollinsPublishers
London

HarperCollins*Publishers*
London

First published in 1999 by HarperCollins*Publishers*

Design and layout © HarperCollins*Publishers* 1999
Text: © Adam Pasco 1999

A catalogue record for this book is available
from the British Library.

ISBN 0-00414103-2

Designed and produced for HarperCollins*Publishers* by
Cooling Brown, Middlesex, England
Editorial: Carole McGlynn, Ann Kay
Design: Arthur Brown, Alistair Plumb, Tish Mills, Pauline Clarke
Photography: Peter Anderson, Steve Gorton

For HarperCollins*Publishers*
Editorial Director: Polly Powell
Managing Editor: Becky Humphries
Production Manager: David Lennox

Colour origination: Colourscan

Printed and bound in Great Britain by Scotprint

Contents

❖

INTRODUCTION

❖

THE KEY TO SUCCESSFUL GARDENING is doing the right thing at the right time, so over the following pages I have set out to provide topical tips and advice through the seasons. Whether you are planning a new garden from scratch or developing an established one, by referring to this guide each week you can plan out what needs to be done, then sow, plant, prune, propagate and cultivate to get the best from your garden.

To help you find the advice you need, the seasonal jobs are divided up to cover the different areas of the garden, from flower border and kitchen garden to lawns, pond and greenhouse. In addition, major seasonal activities are covered in more detail, along with a checklist of jobs to keep your garden problem-free and your plants growing strongly. New gardeners will find this practical guide especially useful, keeping them up-to-date with all the major tasks around the garden, while experienced gardeners can use it more as a reminder.

Why not keep your own personal gardening diary, recording the plans and projects you undertake, keeping notes on crop yields and plant performance,

4

◁ **A PERFECT COMBINATION** *of edible crops and flowers creates an ornamental kitchen garden that is both attractive and abundantly productive.*

◁ CAREFUL
PLANNING *along
with the right choice
of plants and timely
care and attention
will help you develop
a garden that
becomes a real
picture of perfection.*

*and noting all the plants, materials and equipment you buy. This will
quickly build into a complete record of your own garden, to which you
can refer back for guidance each year. The best way to learn about
gardening is, quite simply, to have a go, so turn
these pages to find out what you could be doing in
your garden every day of the year. Most of all, have
fun in your garden, and don't be put off by a few
failures. Your fingers will grow greener by the day,
so happy gardening!*

ADAM PASCO

Early Spring – MARCH

Everything moves up a gear as winter steps into spring, with much to put in place for the coming season. Try and plan out your work, especially seed sowing and propagation plans, setting yourself weekly targets and noting them in a gardening diary.

▽ **TO REJUVENATE AN OVERGROWN** *buddleja, cut back all shoots in early spring to create a tiered branch framework. Prune away all stems that developed last year at their base. New shoots will soon grow.*

THE FLOWER GARDEN

Tree care During dry spells, be sure to water newly planted trees and shrubs. Water well about once a fortnight, and continue this through spring and summer until plants are established.

Clematis Many late flowering clematis need to be pruned hard in late winter or early spring. This includes 'Jackmanii' and types of *C. texensis* and *C. viticella*.

Perennial planting As soon as soil conditions are warmer, this is a good time to plant up new herbaceous beds with perennials. Plant them in groups to create the best effect. It helps to plan the border on paper first, checking the height and spread of individual plants in an encyclopedia so that taller types can be planted at the back, with shorter subjects at the front.

Pruning shrubs On many shrubs the previous season's growth should be pruned back close to its base, to within 2.5cm (1in) of the point it developed

△ SNOWDROPS *that have developed into congested clumps can be lifted and divided as soon as flowering is over.*

6

PLANTING FOR SUMMER COLOUR

◆

LILIES Plant lily bulbs outside where you want them to flower or in pots for planting out later. Many shorter types, especially scented ones, are ideal for patio tubs.

GLADIOLI Plant corms at intervals over the coming months to extend their flowering season. On light soil and in mild areas they can be planted now, but delay planting for a few weeks in colder, wetter areas.

DAHLIAS Tubers can be planted directly outside towards the end of the month. Dig out a large hole, spread out the tuber, then cover with about 10cm (4in) of soil or compost. Protect any emerging shoots from frost by covering with straw or fleece.

CUTTING DOWN TO SIZE

The colourful stems of willows and dogwoods have brightened the winter garden, but these now need pruning hard to encourage a flush of new shoots. Stooling is a pruning technique that keeps vigorous shrubs within bounds where space is limited. All stems are pruned right down to their base, using secateurs or loppers, and although this might look drastic you will soon see a flush of new shoots sprouting out from the woody stubs, providing stems clad in foliage for summer interest and wands of coloured bark next winter.

As well as many shrubby varieties of cornus and salix, other shrubs that can be kept compact and respond well to hard pruning include purple hazel, whitewash bramble, *Cotinus coggygria* and golden-leaved elder. Stems of the summer-flowering *Buddleja davidii* should also be pruned hard down to a woody framework at their base.

Flowering shrubs like lavatera also benefit from very hard pruning. Cut away old growth on perennials like the Russian sage (Perovskia), trim back cotton lavender (Santolina) and remove dead woody stems on fuchsia.

ROSE PRUNING

Most bush roses, especially hybrid tea and floribunda varieties, require an annual prune in early spring. This prevents bushes becoming very woody and bare at the base, encouraging strong new shoots to develop each year which carry flowers through the summer.

Start pruning by removing all dead or diseased stems completely, using loppers to remove portions of old wood. Then look at the size and shape of the bush, and prune out crossing or badly positioned stems. Remove unproductive old stems to make space for the new shoots. Finally, shorten all the existing shoots to shape the bush. In most cases they can simply be shortened by about a third to a half, remembering that weak shoots should be pruned back harder than strong ones, as this encourages more vigorous new growth.

Always prune to just above a bud, using the natural characteristic of shoots to control the resulting shape of the bush. New shoots will grow out in the direction in which the bud is facing.

from last year. Shrubs that can be pruned now include *Hydrangea paniculata*, *Buddleja davidii* and *Caryopteris* x *clandonensis*. Large and unshapely plants of *Brachyglottis* 'Sunshine' can be pruned hard, or old stems shortened back to new side shoots. *Leycestaria formosa* also responds well to hard pruning.

Soil preparation Rake over and prepare sites for sowing hardy annuals later this month or next.

Protection Be prepared to protect the new shoots and developing foliage of tender shrubs and trees from frost and freezing winds. Keep old net curtains or large sheets of fleece handy to spread over and wrap round plants at risk. These include Japanese maples, romneya, caryopteris, ceratostigma, paulownia, some ceanothus, and tender wall plants like *Cytisus battandieri*.

THE KITCHEN GARDEN
Vegetable crops

Seed sowing As soon as soil conditions are suitable start sowing crops outside. These should include parsnips, broad beans, onions, beetroot, carrots, kohl rabi, leeks, peas, radish, mangetout, spinach and turnips.

Onion sets Plant out sets to their required spacing, usually about 10–15cm (4–6in) apart along the row, with rows about 20cm (8in) apart, to allow for hoeing and weeding.

Asparagus New crowns will soon be available to plant.

Choose a vigorous male variety which will not run to seed and plant in deeply cultivated soil. Spread out the roots over a ridge of soil so the crown is planted 5cm (2in) deep.

Shallots Finish planting out shallots in well-drained soil in a sunny site.

Potatoes Plant out early varieties. Seed potatoes will have been chitted on a windowsill, so should have several little shoots sprouting from them.

Salad crops Ensure a regular supply of salads to harvest each week by sowing little and often. The key is to sow a short row of lettuce, radish, salad leaves, spring onions and other crops every week or fortnight, which results in a continuity of crops to harvest through the summer. Sow unusual salad leaves like purslane and salad rocket.

7

◁ **PLANT POTATOES**
in an open, sunny site.
Plant early varieties
about 12cm (5in) deep and
30cm (12in) apart in the row.

▷ **USE CLOCHES** *to warm the soil before sowing early vegetables or flowers, and provide protection from cold and wind for young crops.*

Brassica crops Sow seed of several brassicas in a nursery bed. When the seedlings are large enough to handle, transplant them to their final positions at the proper spacing. Types to sow now include Brussels sprouts, calabrese and summer and autumn cabbage. Sow summer cauliflower under cloches and transplant seedlings from earlier sowings.

Seakale Plant new crowns in spring. Grow plants for a couple of years, feeding them regularly, before they are large enough to cover in winter to form blanched shoots.

Comfrey patch Plant a patch of comfrey in a bright, sunny corner of the kitchen garden. The leaves make an excellent addition to the compost heap, may be spread over the soil round crops as a mulch, or can be used to make a liquid feed. The variety 'Bocking 14' is the most productive comfrey.

Herbs Divide large clumps of chives, separating them into smaller portions to replant. In pots in cold greenhouses or frames sow parsley, sage, chives, dill, lemon balm, sorrel and many others. If you have a heated propagator, sow more tender herbs like basil, coriander, fennel and borage, growing them on in pots ready for planting out in summer.

Fruit crops

Planting Complete planting of new fruit trees and bushes as soon as possible, particularly bare-rooted plants which should always have their roots soaked well before planting.

Strawberries Cover rows with tunnel cloches to encourage earlier flowering and fruiting. Remember to open the sides each day when in bloom, to allow access for bees and pollinating insects.

Gooseberries Finish winter pruning, shortening long side shoots and removing congested stems to create open-centred bushes. This provides better air circulation through the bush, reducing gooseberry mildew disease, and making picking far less painful!

Mulching Spread mulches generously along rows of raspberries and round fruit trees and bushes.

Feeding Continue sprinkling sulphate of potash and general feeds round your fruit, including strawberries.

Peaches and nectarines Keep potted trees in a cold greenhouse until late spring to protect the flowers from frost. Remember to pollinate with a brush.

Fruit trees in lawn Keep grass trimmed away from the base of trees growing in grass, as this can compete for moisture and nutrients. Maintain a clear area about 60–90cm (2–3ft) wide round the trunk, covering the soil with a mulch of compost.

Outdoor vines Complete pruning before vines start into growth.

Pest and disease control Be ready to spray newly emerging leaves with pesticides or fungicides to prevent problems arising this year. Choose products carefully, always following the manufacturer's instructions, and avoid using when plants are in flower as pollinating insects could be harmed.

Frost warning Protect the blooms on cherries, currants and early-flowering fruit from damaging frost with fleece.

LAWN CARE

Moss control Where thick moss is spreading across the lawn, apply a chemical moss killer then thoroughly rake out the dead moss. Improve surface drainage by hollow spiking the lawn to help prevent the problem recurring.

Cutting grass It is still too early to start regular mowing in most areas, but if the weather is very mild and dry, try running the mower over the lawn with blades set high to tidy its appearance.

Lawn edges Re-cut worn or damaged lawn edges. If the edges are in a poor state, aim to replace them with new turf. Alternatively, cut back into good grass using a board and grass cutter to form a clean new edge. Various edging strips are available to put in place to protect edges. Where border plants tumble over the grass, consider putting a row of bricks or paving slabs round the edge as a cutting strip for the plants to spread over. Cut back any invasive plants.

△ **LEAVE A GRASS-FREE** *circle around trees in lawns to prevent competition for water and nutrients. Mulch in spring to retain moisture.*

Raking and scarifying Towards the end of the month, scarify lawns thoroughly, either by hand using a lawn rake or with a powered model. This removes all the debris that accumulates at the soil surface, including moss. Bare patches can be re-seeded later in spring.

POND CARE

Pumps In mild districts, bring pumps out of store and place back in ponds to drive fountains, waterfalls and other moving water features.

Pond heaters Floating electric pond heaters can be removed once the weather warms up and the risk of thick ice developing has passed.

Plant care Any marginal plants that have grown too large can be lifted and divided, replanting young outer portions in smaller groups. Remove invasive plants and thin out any which have become too vigorous for your pond.

Pond weed Keep blanket weed under control, scooping out regularly with a net to prevent it smothering floating plants.

New planting Buy new aquatic plants such as water lilies, iris, sedges and reeds, planting them in aquatic baskets and positioning them on bricks at the correct depth below the water surface.

MULCHING FOR A BETTER GARDEN

❖

A thick layer of compost or similar material spread over the soil helps to suppress annual weeds and conserve moisture. Some mulches break down more quickly than others, being taken down by worms to improve the soil. Others provide an attractive surface and ornamental finishing touch to set off border plants.

WHAT TO USE A wide variety of materials can be used, in particular home-made compost and leafmould, or rotted farmyard manure and mushroom compost. Garden centres sell bark and cocoa shell products by the bag, but larger quantities are available in bulk.

HOW TO MULCH Be generous, spreading a mulch at least 7.5–10cm (3–4in) thick to prevent weed growth. For low-maintenance borders, cover the site with a weed barrier membrane, plant through this into the soil, then cover the membrane with a bark or cocoa shell mulch.

Cocoa shell mulch

Bark mulch

Porous ground matting

Non-porous ground matting

9

▷ **PEACHES IN FLOWER** *under glass should be regularly pollinated by hand using a soft brush, dabbing pollen from one open flower to the next.*

RAISING NEW SHRUBS BY LAYERING

Many shrubs can be propagated by the simple technique of layering a low branch to the ground.

At the point the branch touches the ground, dig out a hole and improve the soil with gritty compost. Make a cut about 2.5cm (1in) long about a third of the way into the stem and towards the shoot tip. Hold the slit open with a matchstick, and dab with hormone rooting powder. Bury in the hole, covering with more gritty compost, water well and hold in place with a large stone or paving slab. Hold the shoot tip upright by tying it to a cane.

Keep the soil watered during dry weather. This layered shoot can take a year, or even longer, to root well, at which time it can be separated from its parent and grown separately.

Shrubs that can be propagated by branch layering during spring include arbutus, evergreen azalea, berberis, camellia, chimonanthus, magnolia, gaultheria and rambling roses. Rhododendrons are easily layered until early autumn, while clematis can be layered during summer.

10

IN THE GREENHOUSE

Peaches With peaches, nectarines and apricots now coming into bloom, protect wall-trained plants on cold nights under a screen of netting or fleece. Bees and other pollinating insects may not be around, so do the job for them by gently dabbing flowers with a soft brush, and transferring pollen from one flower to another. Water if the soil is dry, making sure fruit trees never go short of water during their flowering period.

Fuchsias Pinch out the tips of new shoots once they have produced two or three pairs of leaves. This encourages branching and a better shaped plant which will carry more flowers.

Train up single stems of vigorous, upright varieties to form standards.

Chrysanthemums Continue taking cuttings from new shoots developing on overwintered plants, or buy new stock from specialist growers. Cuttings should be about 5cm (2in) long, and rooted in pots of compost in heated propagators maintained at around 13°C (55°F).

Bedding plants Many varieties of half-hardy summer bedding plants can be sown in heated propagators now. Check the back of seed packets for details.

SOWING VEGETABLES IN THE GREENHOUSE

Several tender crops can be raised from seed now, but they need to be sown in pots or trays and kept in a warm, heated propagator to germinate. These include tomatoes, aubergine, peppers (capsicums), cucumbers. Most will need to be grown in a greenhouse throughout their life, but some varieties can be planted outside in early summer, preferably under cloches at first, to produce crops later in the year. Celery, celeriac and varieties of squash, including marrows and courgettes, can be raised under glass for planting out later in the year.

1 *Fill the seed tray with compost, then level and firm the surface. Sow seed evenly and sparingly.. Use a sieve to cover large seeds thinly with compost.*

2 *Either stand the seed tray in water until compost is moist, or water using a fine rose on the watering can.Cover with a lid and place in a warm position. As soon as seedlings emerge, open vents in lid and keep in a light place.*

Seedlings Prick out seedlings from earlier sowings, spacing them out in large seed trays or planting them individually into small pots.

Damping off disease Some seedlings can collapse and die from damping off. Take steps to prevent the disease by always using clean pots and fresh compost, by sowing thinly and watering with a copper fungicide solution. Never overwater and remove propagator lids to improve ventilation when seedlings have emerged, keeping them in good light.

Primulas Sow a tray of *Primula obconica* to raise flowering pot plants.

Keeping cool On warm days open doors and vents to prevent temperatures rising too high. Remember to close them again in the evening.

Abutilon Prune back large plants grown under glass over the winter to encourage strong growth from the base.

Cacti and succulents Repot large plants during spring in very gritty, loam-based compost. Most prefer terracotta pots, which also provide extra stability.

Taking cuttings If you kept any large tender perennials over the winter, such as fuchsias and marguerites, they will now be putting on strong new growth. These new shoots can be used as cuttings, and rooted individually in pots in a heated propagator.

Tender climbers Sow seed of tender climbing plants like the Chilean glory vine or cup-and-saucer plant.

EARLY SPRING CHECKLIST

❏ Lift, divide and replant large, congested clumps of established perennials every three or four years.

❏ Cover soil in the kitchen garden with polythene or cloches to keep it dry and to warm it up for early sowings.

❏ Pick off the dead flowerheads from spring-flowering bulbs like daffodils and tulips. Scatter fertilizer round each clump.

❏ Cover rhubarb with large pots or buckets to exclude light and force an earlier crop.

❏ Pick off dead flowerheads of winter and spring bedding plants.

❏ Buy in supplies of pots and compost for early sowing and potting. Store bags of compost in the greenhouse so it is already warm for seed sowing.

❏ Open the lids on cold frames each morning to improve ventilation, closing them again each evening.

❏ Control the growth of vigorous spreading herbs, like mint, by cutting back large clumps or by growing them in pots.

❏ Once potted bulbs grown in the home are past their best, plant them outside and give them a liquid feed.

❏ Instead of using cold water from the mains, always leave a full can of water in the greenhouse to take the chill off it before use.

11

Mid-Spring – APRIL

Spring gardens are full of life, vigour, flowers, fresh growth, and a promise of even better to come. Bulbs and blossom steal the show, but the surging growth of new grass indicates a need for regular attention from now on. Seed sowing under glass keeps us busy and the resulting burgeoning trays of seedlings are a testament to the productivity of this season.

△ **FEED ROSES**
now new growth is forming, sprinkling rose fertiliser round each bush, and water it into the soil surface if weather remains dry during spring.

THE FLOWER GARDEN

Gladioli Plant corms in succession from now until the end of spring to extend their flowering season. Place them about 10cm (4in) deep and the same apart, planting in groups of one variety for best effect.

Phormiums Pull off the dead outer leaves, wearing gloves and goggles for protection. Divide congested clumps.

Dahlias Plant sprouting tubers deeply in mild districts, but delay planting tubers by a few weeks in cold areas.

Do not plant out young dahlia plants raised from cuttings until all risk of frost has passed.

Sweet peas Plant out young sweet peas raised from autumn sowings. Pinch out the shoot tip if they have not started to branch naturally. Sow seeds at the base of canes or other vertical supports to grow up for later flowers.

Pampas grass Divide large and congested clumps, or plant out new ones as border features.

Agapanthus Plant bulbs in groups in

▽ **SPRING BULBS**
should be fed and watered during spring to encourage strong growth, leaving the leaves to die down naturally

12

△ CLEMATIS MONTANA *can be left to its own devices unless it grows too large for its allotted space. If it does, prune back long shoots close to their base immediately after flowering.*

large pots, or directly outside in warm and sheltered borders.

Bulbs Sprinkle fertilizer or liquid feed round established drifts of winter- and spring-flowering bulbs like aconites, snowdrops, crocus and narcissus.

Chrysanthemums Continue potting up rooted cuttings, and plant out well-rooted chrysanthemums once they have been hardened off in a cold frame.

Division Many clump-forming and spreading perennials like Russian sage (*Perovskia*) and chrysanthemum can be divided now. Discard the old central portions and replant the young outer pieces in groups.

Indoor bulbs Once pots of bulbs have finished flowering, plant them outside and water well with a liquid feed.

Tubs and containers Remove winter insulation wrapped round patio tubs. Move back containers of shrubs and permanent planting from their sheltered winter homes to their usual positions. Stand containers on pot feet or bricks to ensure good drainage.

THE KITCHEN GARDEN
Vegetable crops

Peas Sow peas and mangetout outside. For a continuity of crops aim to sow at monthly intervals until summer, sowing in bands about 15cm (6in) wide and 5cm (2in) deep. Give tall varieties canes or twigs for support.

Potatoes Plant out maincrop potato varieties. Draw earth up round the stems of newly emerging early varieties every week, and cover with fleece to protect from frost.

Onion sets Plant out as soon as the soil is prepared, spacing them 10–15cm (4–6in) apart in rows about 20cm (8in) apart, allowing room for weeding.

Celery Prepare trenches for planting out young plants raised under glass.

Herbs Several herbs can be sown this month, including parsley, fennel, dill, coriander, marjoram and thyme.

Broad beans Sow a crop now to harvest in the autumn.

Lettuce Start sowing a short row of

13

MID-SPRING PRUNING TASKS

❖

HEATHERS Trim back the dead flower heads on winter-flowering heathers with shears, just cutting into green shoots to shape and tidy the plants. Be careful not to cut back too far into old wood which will not generate new shoots.

FORSYTHIA As soon as flowers have faded, prune back flowering shoots. Trim forsythia hedges with powered hedge cutters, or remove individual shoots with secateurs to create a neat, balanced shrub.

CONIFERS AND TOPIARY With new growth starting and weather improving, give decorative clipped hedges, conifers and topiary the first clip of the year.

FLOWERING CURRANTS To control their size and vigour, varieties of ornamental currant (ribes) need pruning after flowering to remove the old flowered stems and promote new growth that will carry flowers next spring. Prune about a third of stems back hard to encourage new growth from the base, and lightly trim the flowered portion from the rest.

PRUNING SHRUBS Many shrubs flower on shoots produced this year, and not on old growth. If they look tall and untidy after the winter they can be pruned hard now to encourage new growth to develop from the base. Shrubs to prune during spring include hardy fuchsias, romneya, ceratostigma caryopteris and *Hydrangea paniculata*. Some can be pruned back to a slightly larger framework of stems from where new shoots will develop. On shrubs like *Buddleja davidii* and *Leycestaria formosa* leaving some stems of differing lengths will result in a taller, tiered display of flowers this summer.

14

△ **APPLE BLOSSOM** *is at its best now. To ensure a good crop most varieties need to be cross pollinated by another variety flowering at the same time, so grow compatable varieties close to one another.*

lettuce every other week to ensure a regular supply of salad leaves through the summer.

Sprouting seeds A wide range of salad seeds can be sprouted in jars on the kitchen windowsill to use fresh in salads. These include alfalfa, fenugreek, mung beans, rape salad and even chick peas and green lentils. Put a few seeds in a jam jar, rinse with water, then cover the top with muslin and leave upside down to drain. Repeat rinsing and draining daily. Seedlings soon sprout and will be ready to eat in a few days. Set up the number of jars and quantities needed for your family requirements.

Carrots Sow under cloches or outside for small salad carrots, or later for maincrop varieties. Sowing sparingly at intervals along the row avoids the need for thinning, which can attract carrot root fly. Covering rows with fleece after sowing, buried along the edges, also prevents attack from carrot root fly. A few varieties, like 'Sytan' and 'Flyaway' also claim resistance to this pest.

Crops to sow outdoors Sow beetroot, carrots, radish, kohl rabi, lettuce, spring onions, peas, spinach, swede and turnip, and brassicas like sprouting broccoli, kale, cabbage and Brussels sprouts. Cover rows with cloches.

To sow in pots Sow courgette, marrow, squash, tomato, sweetcorn and French beans in pots indoors. In warm districts some crops can also be sown outdoors, under cloches.

Strawberries Cover the rows of crops with tunnel cloches, opening the sides each day to allow access for pollinating insects to reach the early flowers as soon as they open.

Raspberries New canes will be growing now. Remove any coming up between rows or in paths, and thin out the rest to leave them spaced about 15cm (6in) apart.

Peaches Thin out heavy crops on fan-trained trees under glass.

Pruning plums Avoid pruning plums and cherries in winter as this can spread disease. Now their sap is rising and they are starting into growth, prune to remove dead and damaged shoots, thin congested growth and tie in new shoots.

Mulching Spread a mulch of compost around fruit trees and bushes to conserve soil moisture and keep down the weeds.

TRANSPLANTING BRASSICAS

Transplant young seedlings of cabbages and other brassicas sown in seed beds earlier in the year. Choose an overcast day if possible, and water plants well the day before. Lift carefully with a hand fork and transplant to well-prepared soil at their correct spacing where they will grow to maturity. Always firm soil round brassica roots. Water in well and place a collar of old carpet underlay round the stem of each to prevent female cabbage root fly gaining access to lay her eggs.

CHOOSING THE BEST PLANTS TO BUY

To ensure that you always buy the very best plants, observe these rules when visiting the nursery or garden centre.

1. Aim to shop at the end of the week when stocks of fresh plants are in place for the weekend. You are more likely to get personal advice if you shop during the week when it is quieter.

2. Check that plants look strong, healthy, vigorous and well shaped.

3. Avoid plants with a thick layer of moss or weeds growing on the surface of the compost.

4. Check that thick roots are not growing through the bottom of the pot, which is a clear indication that an old plant has become pot-bound.

5. The compost should be moist. Never buy plants that have dried out.

6. Check that plants have no visible signs of pests or diseases.

7. Make sure plants are labelled with a variety name and cultural instructions.

8. Try to choose plants that come with a money-back or replacement guarantee.

Feeding Sprinkle fertilizer round trees and bushes and rake into the soil.

Disease control Mildew diseases attack apples, gooseberries, currants and other fruits. Planting disease-resistant varieties is one way to avoid them, but protect susceptible varieties by spraying with a systemic fungicide.

Frost protection Keep netting or fleece handy to cover fruits in flower on cold nights to protect them from frost.

Greenfly control To reduce the spread of greenfly by ants on fruit trees, wrap a sticky collar round the trunk and stake.

LAWN CARE

Mowing Begin a weekly mowing regime, collecting all the cuttings as you mow. Keep the blades set quite high at the start of the season, lowering it a little at a time as grass growth increases over the weeks.

Feeding Apply a high-nitrogen lawn

Δ **HOLLOW-TINE SPIKERS** *remove entire cores of soil each time they are pressed down into the soil. Sweep up the deposited soil, then brush grit into the holes left in the lawn, to improve both aeration and drainage.*

feed to all grass areas to get growth off to a good start. Water in granular formulations if it does not rain.

Seeding and patching Thin and worn areas of lawn can be seeded or over-

15

◁ **FLOWERING CURRANT** *puts on a glorious display in spring, but as soon as the last flowers fade, very old shoots need pruning back hard.*

Scarifying Use a tined rake or powered scarifier to rake out moss and thatch that has accumulated deep down in the lawn near the soil surface.

Moss Treat areas of moss with a moss killer, then rake out the dead moss. Take steps to improve soil drainage and relieve compaction by forking over the lawn with a hollow-tined aerator. Brush sharp sand or grit down into the hollow cores to produce drainage channels.

POND CARE

Tidy-up Collect dead stems or foliage from pond or marginal plants, scooping them out of the water with a small net if necessary. Take care not to damage butyl-lined ponds.

Feeding plants Push fertilizer pellets down into the compost of established water lilies and other aquatic plants growing in baskets.

Pumps and fountains Pumps stored in the garage over winter can be placed back in ponds now. Replace old filters

and attach to fountains and waterfalls.

Filtration systems Run a pond filtration system, such as those containing ultra-violet lights, to kill algae and purify the water. These are simple to install and are an effective way of keeping pond water clear.

Water lilies Divide large plants now. Lift the whole aquatic basket from the pond, remove the water lily, and cut into sections with a knife. Make sure each piece has shoots and roots attached. Replant into baskets of fresh aquatic compost and cover this with a layer of gravel. Gently lower back onto their shelf in the pool.

IN THE GREENHOUSE

Shading Temperatures can soar under glass on hot days, so put up shading blinds and screens, or apply shade paint to the outside of the glass.

Ventilation Open vents each morning, closing them again in the evening. On very hot days also leave the door ajar to provide extra ventilation.

Cold protection If frost is forecast, cover plants on staging with sheets of fleece or sheets of newspaper for extra protection from cold, removing them in the morning.

Seedlings Continue pricking out seedlings as soon as they are large enough to handle.

Cuttings Take cuttings from new growth of dahlias, fuchsias and many house plants, including leaf cuttings from saintpaulia and *Begonia rex*.

Potting on Always choose a pot just one size larger when potting on, leaving an extra 1cm (½in) or so of fresh compost round the rootball. Always use the same type of compost as before,

sown to thicken up growth. Scratch over the area with a rake, sprinkle with seed, cover with a thin layer of potting compost, and water well. Small patches can be covered with a piece of clear polythene, pegged in position, to keep birds off. Remove as soon as the grass has germinated.

16 **Weeding** Dig out problem weeds like daisies, dandelions and buttercups.

STARTING A NEW LAWN

❖

- With damper weather and regular showers in spring, this is a good time to raise new lawns from seed or to lay turf. Always prepare the site well, ensuring the area is free from weeds.

- Once you have dug over the soil, consolidate by walking over it on your heels, raking it level and mixing in fertilizer. Sow seed at the stated rate but no thicker, as sowing too

thickly results in weak, congested growth that is prone to disease.

- Keep off a newly sown or laid lawn until well established, although you will need to give it an occasional cut with the mower blades set quite high. Ensure the grass never goes short of water in the period while it is establishing. Spot treat any weeds that develop in your new lawn.

△ **ALPINE SINK GARDENS** *can be planted at any time of year, but look their best in spring. Choose a range of alpines, including sempervivums and sedum, and plant them in gritty, free-draining compost.*

keeping plants growing in a loam-based compost in loam, for instance.

Primulas Sow seed of several primulas which can be grown as pot plants, including *Primula obconica*, *P. kewensis* and *P. sinensis*.

Growing bags Plant cucumbers, peppers and early tomatoes into growing bags in heated greenhouses.

Nerines Continue watering and feeding nerines growing in pots for a few more weeks before reducing the watering to allow the leaves to die down. Give plants a complete rest over the summer, leaving them in a warm position under the greenhouse staging.

Plants by post As soon as young plants are delivered, open boxes, water any dry plants and stand in good light. Contact the nursery if plants were damaged in the post. Pot up as soon as possible.

GREEN MANURES TO SOW
❖

Where space in a border will remain vacant for anything from a few weeks to a few months, sow a green manure crop. This will produce fresh, leafy growth that can be chopped up and dug in to improve the soil. Some green manures also have nitrogen fixing bacteria in nodules in their roots which take nitrogen from the air, and release it to following crops for them to feed on. It is best to plant young plants into soil improved with green manures, as the decaying vegetation can inhibit seed germination. If sowing new crops, leave at least a month before sowing. Green manures to choose from which fix nitrogen include tares, trefoil, fenugreek, clover and lupins. Those that don't include fast-growing mustard, phacelia and buckwheat.

MID-SPRING CHECKLIST

❏ Move young plants from greenhouses and windowsills into cold frames to get them gradually used to cooler outside conditions before planting out.

❏ Hoe borders regularly to kill germinating weed seedlings and dig up emerging perennial weeds.

❏ Sprinkle a generous handful of fertilizer round every flowering shrub, raking it into the soil surface if possible.

❏ Apply a residual weedkiller to gravel paths and drives.

❏ Spread a mulch of bark or compost round shrubs and fruit bushes to suppress weed growth and conserve soil moisture.

❏ Plant up troughs with alpine plants to enjoy this spring.

❏ Keep vegetable plots tidy, removing leaves and debris that could encourage slugs and snails. Dig up and destroy old brassica plants that could be harbouring the grubs of cabbage root fly.

❏ Give acid loving ericaceous plants a liquid feed of iron sequestrene.

❏ Be on the lookout for the first signs of pests, like greenfly. Pick off or treat pests right away.

❏ Every garden should have sufficient compost bins to recycle all its waste prunings, lawn mowing and other debris. If not, invest in extra bins now so you can make more compost this year.

17

Late Spring – MAY

There is hardly a moment to spare this month, with plants to propagate from cuttings for summer displays and vegetable crops and salads to sow outside. Mowing, trimming, weeding and planting all form part of the weekly action plan, and with warmer weather boosting new growth, all plants will benefit from a good feed and more regular watering.

THE FLOWER GARDEN

Plant supports Use canes to support the developing stems of herbaceous perennials, particularly floppy ones like peonies and tall subjects like delphiniums. Either stake individual stems and flower spikes, or surround a clump with several canes. Join them together with garden twine and place eye protectors on the tops of canes.

Feeding Give all acid-loving garden shrubs, like rhododendrons, azaleas, pieris and camellias a feed with a fertilizer formulated specifically for them, such as iron sequestrene, to prevent leaves turning yellow. All spring-flowering bulbs will benefit from a liquid feed. Apply fertilizer round conifers, perennials, established shrubs and along the base of hedges.

▽ **USE COLD FRAMES** *to harden off summer bedding before planting outside in late May.*

Seed sowing In a nursery bed, sow seeds of wallflowers and forget-me-nots and of biennial flowers like honesty and Canterbury bells. These can be transplanted to their flowering position later in the year. At the end of this month sow nasturtiums outside.

Forking borders Regularly spike over border soil with a fork to relieve compaction and remove weeds. Fork in a general fertilizer round established plants at the same time.

Perennials Spread a layer of well-rotted compost round perennials. Watch out for slugs and snails, removing any you find, or use a chemical control.

Hardy annuals Continue sowing directly into borders wherever you would like them to flower. Thin out seedlings from earlier sowings to their desired spacing.

Frost protection Many summer bedding plants are frost-tender, so do not plant outside until the all risk of a late frost has passed. Make sure plants have been hardened off by gradually acclimatizing them to outdoor conditions. Open cold frames fully each day, or move plants out of the greenhouse for the day, taking them back in again every evening.

Euphorbias Prune out old flower stems towards the end of this month to provide more space for the developing stems. Wear gloves, as the sap of euphorbias is a skin irritant.

Hellebores It is useful to leave the old flowers on some hellebores, like *H. niger* and *H. orientalis* to allow them to self-seed. On others like *H. argutifolius*, however, the resulting seedlings come

We run the risk of congestion in flower borders this month as spring-flowering bulbs are still growing strongly where summer bedding soon needs to be planted. Bulbs need their foliage now to help build up food reserves for next spring. Leave the foliage intact for at least six weeks after flowering, longer if possible. It can then be cut off at soil level. Leave deeply planted bulbs in place, planting bedding over the top. Lift shallow-planted bulbs in clumps with as much root and soil as possible and replant in a quiet corner of the garden. Apply liquid feed and allow to die down naturally. Lift and store for the summer.

◁ **CONTINUE POTTING** *bedding plants into larger pots, growing them on in the greenhouse. Don't plant out until all risk of frost has passed.*

ready to plant out when risk of frost has passed. Prepare planting sites by digging in plenty of compost, and hammer tall, thick stakes in position ready for training and supporting tall varieties.

Climbing plants

Planting Finish planting out sweet peas, and tie in new growth. Plant out annual climbers raised under glass at the end of this season, positioning them near fences, trellis or other supports for them to cling to and climb.

Training Tie in new growth and flower stems on clematis, directing their stems into areas where you would like blooms. Tie in the new shoots of honeysuckle and climbing roses, particularly those trained over arches or pergolas, so that they hang down gracefully.

Rose care

Pests Look out for signs of greenfly on the shoot tips which can damage new leaves and growth. Rub off by hand or spray with a soap-based insecticide.

Feeding Sprinkle a generous handful of rose fertilizer round the base of all roses.

- Once flowering has finished, cut all the stems of flowering almond (*Prunus triloba*) right down to their base to encourage new growth.

- Prune broom (*Genista*) after flowering to shape the plants and prevent them growing lanky, shortening the stems but never cutting back into old wood.

- Tie in new growth of wall-trained pyracantha to their supports, and prune out any unwanted shoots that are developing directly into or away from the wall.

Hoe shallowly into the soil surface if possible, taking care not to harm roots, or simply water well before covering with a mulch of compost.

Diseases If your rose varieties are susceptible to mildew, black spot and rust, try picking off leaves showing signs of infection to prevent it spreading. Alternatively, start a regular spray programme, using a rose fungicide.

Standard roses Check supports are sound, and replace if damaged or unstable. Loosen ties which could be damaging the stem. Replace if worn.

up like weeds, so remove flowerheads before they spill their seed.

Dividing plants Lift and divide primulas, polyanthus and forget-me-nots now. Dig up whole plants and tease them apart, ready for planting in a nursery bed to grow on to a larger size before planting out later in the year.

Dahlias Harden off rooted cuttings,

19

To ensure a continuity of cropping for the longest season possible, it is important to make several sowings at intervals during spring and early summer. Many crops, especially salads, can be sown little and often to produce sufficient crops to meet family needs. Lettuce, radish, spinach, turnips and salad leaves may be sown fortnightly. Sow in short rows, perhaps only 60cm (2ft) long, of each variety, to grow the crops you need. With other crops, like maincrop peas and mangetout, two or three sowings at monthly intervals will be needed to provide succession.

△ MAKE REGULAR SOWINGS *of lettuce and other salads. Once seedlings have germinated, thin out to leave plants evenly spaced along the row, providing the crop with room to grow and fully mature.*

THE KITCHEN GARDEN
Vegetable crops

Mangetout Continue sowing mangetout peas in shallow trenches about 15cm (6in) wide and 5cm (2in) deep, spacing the seeds about 7.5cm (3in) apart across the area. Cover with soil, firm it down and water in the seeds. Provide twiggy supports for taller-growing varieties.

Asparagus Cut spears as they develop, using a long knife to sever them well below the soil surface.

Rhubarb Continue pulling rhubarb regularly and water clumps during very dry weather to encourage new growth.

Broad beans Pinch out the tips of broad bean stems to remove the soft growth which blackfly find so attractive.

Potatoes Complete planting of maincrop varieties. Earth up stems of early varieties to increase yields.

Brussels sprouts Transplant young plants raised from earlier sowings to their final permanent rows, leaving about 60cm (2ft) between plants.

Planting out When all risk of frost has passed, plant out tender crops like outdoor tomatoes and ridge cucumbers, celeriac and celery raised under glass.

Seed sowing Once all risk of frost has passed, sow runner beans, dwarf French beans, ridge cucumbers, courgettes and sweetcorn outside. Cover with cloches until crops are well established. Sow beetroot, spinach, Chinese cabbage, winter cauliflower, New Zealand spinach, calabrese, cauliflower, chicory, endive, kohl rabi, lettuce, spring onions, peas, radish, swedes, turnips and chicory.

Fruit crops

Strawberries Spread straw along rows and under swelling strawberry fruits to keep them off the soil, reducing the risk of attack by slugs and getting covered in soil. Pick fruits from early strawberries growing under cloches.

Raspberries Tie in new growth and thin congested canes to leave them spaced about 15cm (6in) apart along

△ MULCH STRAWBERRIES *while still small with straw or with strawberry mats to keep the fruit clean. Pinch off the runners unless they are needed for propagation and net against birds.*

the row. Hoe off any raspberry suckers growing up between the rows.

Gooseberries Thin fruits, using the crop for cooking. Remove every alternate fruit along stems, leaving more room for remaining ones to swell and develop. Keep spraying against powdery mildew if this is a problem.

Suckers Remove suckers on fruit trees growing up from their rootstocks.

Mulching Spread a thick layer of garden compost round fruit trees and bushes to conserve soil moisture.

Fan-trained fruits Regularly tie in branches of fan-trained fruit trees like peach, nectarine, plum, cherry and damson, extending the fan framework to cover a wall or fence.

Outdoor grape vines Pinch out the tips of all side' shoots growing from the main rod framework once they have started developing flower trusses. Tie shoots in to their supports.

Bird control Cover fruit cages with netting, or drape netting over fruit bushes and strawberries to keep birds away from developing fruits.

Disease control Continue a regular spraying programme with a suitable garden fungicide to control powdery mildew, apple scab and other diseases.

Codling moth control Hang pheromone traps in apple trees from late spring to attract and catch the male codling moth. Remember to replace the pheromone capsule after a few weeks, when it has become exhausted.

CROPS IN GROWING BAGS

❖

Even where space is limited, a number of crops can be grown in compost-filled growing bags. Traditionally used in greenhouses for tomatoes, they can be used to grow many other crops, including peppers, cucumbers, salads, aubergines, strawberries, or herbs, all of which can be planted in an unheated greenhouse now. Growing bags are also useful for balcony and roof gardens. To make watering easier, stand the bag on a gravel tray and cut slits in the base of the bag to carry wicks to take water from the reservoir to the compost. Remember that growing bags contain little fertilizer, and from about a month after planting, crops will need a weekly liquid feed. Keep the reservoir permanently topped up with water. Tie developing plants to frames, strings or other supports as they grow.

LAWN CARE

Cutting height Gradually lower the height of the blades on your mower as grass growth gets stronger. Start by cutting this season at a height of about 2.5cm (1in) or higher for rough areas, and lower the blades progressively over the coming weeks to a height as low as 1.25cm (½in) for fine-quality lawns.

Feeding Apply lawn feed in some form. Quick-acting liquid feeds which are high in nitrogen can be applied with a watering can, or slow-release granular feeds applied evenly with a wheeled lawn spreader.

Moss control Renovate lawns that are full of moss and dead grass. Apply a moss killer, then thoroughly rake out the dead moss and the accumulated debris by hand or by using a powered lawn rake.

Repairs Areas where grass growth is very thin can be over-sown with grass seed, raking it into the soil surface and covering with a fine sprinkling of compost. Small patches can be covered with clear polythene, pegged down to keep the birds off until the grass seed has germinated.

Lawn weeds Dig out individual weeds by hand, or treat large areas of spreading weeds with a herbicide specially formulated for lawns.

◁ **GIVE LAWNS A BOOST** *by applying liquid lawn feed. For large areas, attach a fertiliser dilutor to the end of your hose pipe. This can be used for feeding lawns and flower borders.*

21

POND CARE

Water lilies This is a good time to divide large plants. Lift baskets from their pond shelf, empty the contents and divide clumps up into individual portions, each with root and shoot attached. Replant into fresh aquatic compost and gradually lower back onto their shelf in stages as the plant grows.

Green algae Filamentous algae soon spread through ponds, covering the surface and strangling plants. Remove regularly by twisting onto a stick or rake, adding this to the compost heap. Take care not to damage butyl liners.

New plants Add oxygenating plants to ponds to improve the quality of the water. Plant deep-water aquatics like water hawthorn (*Aponogeton*), water lilies (*Nymphaea*) and floating heart (*Nymphoides*).

General advice Top up water levels whenever necessary. Use a small net to scoop out accumulated debris or remove floating duckweed.

▽ AQUATIC PLANTS *should be planted in plastic baskets, then lowered down into the pool to rest on a shelf or pile of bricks in the base.*

22

IN THE GREENHOUSE

Fuchsias Pinch out the shoot tips to encourage branching. Remember that while this helps form bushier plants it does delay flowering.

Grape vines Carefully thin out large bunches with finely pointed scissors, removing small or damaged grapes. Pinch out the tips of long shoots a few leaves beyond developing bunches.

Begonias Tubers started into growth earlier in the year can now be potted up individually into 15cm (6in) pots.

Vine weevil Be vigilant for any signs of adult or larval damage from vine weevil, and treat compost in pots and borders by drenching with a biological pest control nematode if any are found.

Watering Most plants are demanding more water now, so check those in the greenhouse daily. Add liquid feed weekly.

Cuttings Select non-flowering shoots of new growth on hydrangeas to use as cuttings. Take cuttings of alpines. Pot on any cuttings that rooted earlier.

Seedlings Prick out seedlings once large enough to handle, and pot on rooted cuttings and young plants.

Shading Prevent greenhouses getting too hot on bright days by shading the glass on the south side and the roof, in particular, with shade paint, netting or roller blinds. Open doors and ventilators each morning, or fit automatic vent openers. Keep heaters on stand-by to use on cold nights.

Hardening off On warm days, move pots and trays of bedding plants, dahlias, chrysanthemums, and tender vegetables outside or into frames to

◁ PICK OFF FADED BLOOMS *from azaleas and rhododendrons to prevent them setting seed. Also give all plants a generous liquid feed.*

HANGING BASKETS AND CONTAINERS

❖

If you have a greenhouse or a conservatory, try to plant up containers and baskets with summer bedding early in the season. This allows small plants to get established and reach a larger size before being put into their permanent home for the summer months. A wide variety of half-hardy bedding plants and tender perennials – like fuchsias, pelargoniums and argyranthemums – will now be available at garden centres, in addition to trailing begonias and other flowers. Be generous when planting containers, choosing large pots and putting in plenty of plants to create the most impressive displays.

harden them off and acclimatize them to outside conditions.

Cucumbers Pinch out the tips of side shoots two leaves beyond developing fruits. Stop any side shoots not carrying flowers once they have reached a length of about 60cm (2ft). Remove the main shoot tip when it reaches the roof. Feed cucumbers regularly.

Tomatoes Tie leading shoots to canes or supports each week, and pinch out side shoots, which can grow at each leaf up the stem. Tap flowers daily as they open to encourage pollination and a better fruit set. Never let plants go short of water, and feed twice weekly with a high potash tomato fertilizer.

Bulbs at rest Reduce watering of pots of nerine, lachenalia, veltheimea and freesia to allow them to die down for a

summer rest. Stand under the staging.

Chrysanthemums Keep potting on cuttings and young plants into larger sized pots as their roots grow. To encourage well-branched plants to form, pinch out the shoot tips. The number of shoots retained to flower depends on the variety being grown.

LATE SPRING CHECKLIST

❐ Pick off the faded flowers from camellias, rhododendrons, azaleas and magnolias.

❐ Trim privet hedges regularly to keep them tidy and well shaped.

❐ Support the developing flower stems of tall lilies, and use canes to support gladioli in exposed gardens.

❐ Hoe regularly on dry days to prevent weed seedlings getting established.

❐ Apply a long-lasting weedkiller to gravel paths and drives.

❐ Treat the new growth of emerging perennial weeds with herbicide.

❐ Be considerate of birds that may be nesting in hedges or shrubs.

❐ Watch out for greenfly or other pests on shrubs, and treat if required.

❐ Finish planting perennials, watering in with a liquid feed.

❐ Keep rock gardens and alpine containers tidy, cutting off dead flower stems when they are over.

❐ Repair damaged edges to lawns.

❐ Keep newly purchased plants in a quarantine area of the greenhouse for a few days in case they are carrying pests.

◁ TIE CUCUMBERS *to upright canes or gently twist their stems around strings suspended from the greenhouse roof.*

Early Summer – JUNE

Everything is growing strongly now, including the weeds, and the priority is to get everything planted up ready for the summer displays and crops. As temperatures increase so does the need for daily watering, so find time while relaxing in your garden each evening to potter round the plot with a watering can.

Solanum crispum

THE FLOWER GARDEN

Summer bedding Complete planting out of tender bedding plants, either in pots and containers or directly in borders, watering them in with a solution of liquid feed.

Training climbers Tie in to walls, trellis and supports the new growth of climbers and shrubs like honeysuckle, roses, clematis and *Solanum crispum*.

Cuttings Plant out chrysanthemums and dahlias raised from cuttings, giving each a strong stake to support the flower stems as they grow. Pinch out the main shoot tip on early-flowering chrysanthemums to encourage them to produce well branched plants.

Canna lilies Plants grown in pots in the greenhouse can be planted outside, providing taller growing accent plants within summer bedding displays.

Layering shrubs Raise new plants of cytisus, deciduous azaleas, magnolias and other shrubs by layering low-growing shoots of young growth to soil level. Keep soil round shoots layered earlier in the year constantly moist.

Supporting Continue tying flower spikes to canes on tall-growing perennials, like delphiniums.

Spraying roses Rose varieties which always succumb to mildew or black spot should be sprayed with a suitable fungicide at regular intervals throughout the summer. Replace disease-prone roses with new disease-resistant varieties in the future. Where greenfly are also a problem, apply a combined insecticide and fungicide formulated for roses.

Disbudding roses For extra-large rose blooms, perhaps for cutting or for exhibition, remove any buds developing at the side of the main terminal bloom on each shoot.

Feeding Sprinkle granules of a general fertilizer round flowering plants and shrubs. Hoe into the soil surface and water in if the weather remains dry. Alternatively, give plants a generous soaking with liquid feed every fortnight.

Clematis Prune large and overgrown *C. montana* this month, cutting back hard to encourage new growth.

24

▷ **FILL GAPS IN BORDER** *with colourful bedding plants like pelargoniums and Gypsophila myralis. Planted in early summer, they will bloom till autumn, outlasting the perennial daisies.*

- Marrows, courgettes, pumpkins and squashes can be planted outside now. Make a slight hollow in the ground to plant into, mounding the soil up round the young plant in a ring so that water poured into this depression runs directly to the roots.

- With outdoor tomatoes and other plants with a high demand for water, sink an empty 7.5–10cm (3–4in) plastic pot into the soil next to each plant. Watering straight into the pot directs water to the plant roots instead of just wetting the soil surface.

- Add a high-potash tomato fertilizer to the water once a week throughout the summer. Cover the soil surface round plants with a mulch of garden compost both to conserve moisture and to prevent the growth of weed seedlings.

◁ TRAIN SHRUBS *and climbers to walls and fences, tying in new growth to horizontal wires fixed at regular intervals to screws.*

25

THE KITCHEN GARDEN
Vegetable crops

Beans Plant out runner beans or dwarf French beans raised in pots in the greenhouse, or sow directly outside in early June for a later crop.

Potatoes Draw soil up round the stems to encourage them to root into this ridge of soil and develop a larger crop. Sprinkle a general fertilizer along the rows, mixing this into the soil as earthing up proceeds.

Outdoor cucumbers Plant out ridge cucumbers in cold frames. In warmer regions they can often be grown successfully outside in a sunny site.

Planting out Plant out leeks, self-blanching celery, marrows, courgettes, squashes and pumpkins.

Tomatoes Both bush and cordon tomatoes can also be planted out now risk of frost has passed. Tie cordon tomatoes to thick stakes standing at least 90cm (3ft) tall. Train these up as a single stem, removing their side shoots, while bush tomato varieties can be left to scramble over the ground unchecked.

Broad beans Pinch out the soft tips of broad bean plants to reduce the risk of attack by blackfly.

Chicory Sow chicory as soon as possible, growing roots that can be lifted and potted next winter and forced to raise chicons for winter salads.

Salad sowings Sow a few seeds of salad crops like lettuce, radish and salad leaves every fortnight during summer.

Crops to sow Other crops to sow this month for a late harvest include endive, swede, beetroot, carrots, chicory, marrow, kohl rabi, purslane, New Zealand spinach, swede, sweet corn, Chinese cabbage, turnip and cauliflower. Thin out seedlings from earlier sowings to their final spacing.

PRUNING SHRUBS

- Prune late spring- and early summer- flowering shrubs like philadelphus, weigela, pyracantha, ceanothus, kerria, Berberis darwinii, escallonia and deutzia immediately after flowering.

- Although pruning is not needed every year, it encourages new growth from the base and prevents shrubs becoming tall but open and bare at the bottom.

- A system of renewal pruning can be used for many shrubs, cutting out about one in three shoots to promote fresh new shoots to grow up and replace them.

- On wall-trained shrubs, tie in new shoots to support wires or trellis. Remove shoots growing directly away from, or straight into, the wall. Healthy new shoot tips of many shrubs can be used as cuttings rooted in pots of compost.

- After pruning, give shrubs a generous soaking with liquid feed and cover the soil round them with a mulch to conserve moisture.

△ PRUNE BACK *any philadelphus stems that carried flowers once blooms fall.*

Fruit crops

Bird control Cover gooseberries, currants, strawberries and soft fruits with netting to keep birds away. Weave a cane into the base edge of the netting and peg down to the ground to prevent birds getting underneath.

Strawberries Spread a straw mulch along strawberry rows just under the foliage and developing fruits to keep them off the soil.

Gooseberries Pick small gooseberries to thin out heavy crops, leaving the remaining fruits well spaced out along the branches to continue growing to a larger size. Use these small, immature fruits for cooking.

Thinning apples Apple trees may have set a very heavy crop. Some of these will fall naturally, but you can help by picking off malformed, damaged or diseased fruits, or those showing signs of pest attack.

Plums Thin out fruit to leave them spaced about 5–7.5cm (2–3in) apart.

Figs Tie in the shoots of fan-trained figs growing against warm walls. Pinch out the tips of all side shoots once they have produced five leaves.

Raspberry beetle If you have found small maggots in fruits in the past, consider spraying fruitlets with a suitable insecticide now to control the pest. Also spray blackberry, loganberry and other cane fruits. Control aphids, too, which spread debilitating viruses.

LAWN CARE

Mowing Cut lawns at least once a week now grass is growing strongly, and twice a week for a better finish on fine lawns.

Clippings Recycle grass cuttings, composting them in a bin or using them as a mulch round trees and bushes.

Length of cut If the weather is very dry, leave grass longer than normal to help it withstand drought.

Watering Do not waste water on your lawn by leaving lawn sprinklers

EARLY-SUMMER PLANT PROPAGATION

- Lift and divide congested clumps of flag iris after flowering. Dig up the whole clump, cutting away old or damaged pieces of rhizome, and replant healthy individual flags into newly enriched soil. Keep the rhizome resting at the soil surface so that it can bake in the sun. In exposed sites the leaves, or flags, may be reduced in size.

- The soft new growth to be found on many shrubs makes ideal material for softwood cuttings. These will quickly root in a heated propagator or greenhouse. Try taking cuttings from hydrangea, cotoneaster, weigela and philadelphus among many others.

- Propagate only from healthy non-flowering shoots. Most root better if the cut end is dipped in a hormone-rooting compound which usually also contains a fungicide to prevent the cutting from rotting.

- Individual cuttings can be placed in small pots of moist, gritty compost. Cover pots with clear plastic bottles or bags, held in place with an elastic band. Once roots can be seen growing through the bottom of the pot, remove the cover. Keep in a bright position.

△ THE MOST CONVENIENT *way of neatening the edges of a lawn after mowing is to use these manual shears. Their long handles enable you to do the job without bending.*

running. Recycle your domestic water, pouring bowls of washing-up or bath water onto the lawn.

Lawn weeds Dig out or spot-treat individual weeds, like dandelions. Badly weed-infested lawns may need treating more thoroughly with a liquid or granular weedkiller. Water well if it does not rain within a few days of applying.

Feeding Feed grass with a high-nitrogen lawn feed. Liquid formulations are often quicker to apply than powders and get straight to work, while some granular formulations have a longer-lasting action to feed grass all season.

Lawn mowers If your mower is not cutting efficiently, adjust or sharpen the blades, or have the mower serviced.

▷ DUCKWEED *consists of two tiny leaves that float on the water's surface, with short, trailing roots. It multiplies rapidly, forming mats that smother the pond. Skim them off with a fish net.*

POND CARE

General advice Top up water levels as they fall in hot weather. Use a child's small fishing net to scoop out duckweed and filamentous algae. Tidy the pond margins regularly, to prevent dead flower stems and leaves accumulating, and falling into the water.

Plant cover It is essential to achieve the right balance in a garden pond. Aim to cover about a half to two-thirds of the surface area with floating plants, like water lilies. Plant more aquatics in baskets now if this is necessary to achieve better cover.

Wildlife safety Make sure you place a small ramp into steep-sided, formal pools and water features so that small mammals, like hedgehogs, can climb out if they accidentally fall in. Informal ponds made using a liner can be left with a pebble beach along one edge.

HOME COMPOSTING
❖

Virtually all garden waste can be recycled into compost, along with old vegetables, fruit, peelings and egg shells from the kitchen. If possible, invest in two compost heaps, so that while one is rotting down fresh material can be added to the other. A totally enclosed bin with a lid is far better than an open one with slatted sides. Aim to mix together a variety of materials as they are added to the heap. Avoid putting in thick layers of lawn mowings, for instance, which can form a soggy mass. Add a little at a time between layers of clippings and other waste. Shred thick and woody material before composting. Mix a biological compost activator into the heap to speed up the composting process, and make sure the material never dries out. Water if necessary.

27

GROWING TREES AND SHRUBS IN TUBS

❖

- Both evergreen and flowering shrubs and small trees, like Japanese maples, make perfect subjects for patio tubs. They are mobile, so displays can be varied, and plants taken with you when you move home.

- Choose large containers at least 35cm (14in) across and the same depth, making sure they have drainage holes in the base. Add a layer of crocks before filling with a soil-based compost. However, for acid-loving shrubs like camellias and blueberries, use an ericaceous compost. Plant, leaving a 5cm (2in) gap between compost level and the top of the pot to make watering easier. Shrubs will

require almost daily watering at the height of summer, plus a liquid feed each week. Stand pots on bricks or feet to improve drainage.

- Fruit trees can also be grown in large tubs. Choose compact varieties of peach, cherry, plum, apple and other fruits specially recommended for this purpose, often grown on a dwarf rootstock. If you only have space for a single tree, choose a self-fertile variety, otherwise a pollinator will be needed to guarantee a crop.

▽ TREE FERNS *make striking architectural features on their own, ideal for a shaded position on a patio or close to buildings.*

IN THE GREENHOUSE

Keeping cool Open greenhouse doors and vents each morning to keep temperatures down, but close them at night. Hang shade netting or blinds over the south side of greenhouses, or paint with shading paint.

Feeding Continue feeding plants in pots and growing bags at least once a week. It is sometimes better to use a liquid feed at half-strength twice a week to ensure plants in containers never go short of nutrients.

Cuttings Take cuttings from coleus, fancy-leaf begonias, African violets and other house plants. Also propagate fuchsias and Regal pelargoniums.

Pinks Take cuttings of non-flowering shoots about 10cm (4in) long, pushing several into small pots of compost.

Begonias Pot on tuberous begonias and support tall plants with canes. Feed begonias and gloxinias regularly.

Seed sowing Sow flowering pot plant varieties of *Primula malacoides*, *Primula sinensis*, calceolaria and cineraria.

Whitefly under glass Hang yellow

△ REGULARLY PINCH *out the tips of coleus shoots to encourage bushy growth, and remove any flowers immediately they appear.*

28

sticky cards in the greenhouse or conservatory to trap whitefly. Release the parasitic wasp (*Encarsia*) as soon as whitefly are seen, to prevent the problem getting out of hand.

PEST CONTROL

Aphids Heavy infestations of greenfly may need treating with a soap-based spray or insecticide.

Slugs and snails Collect slugs or snails you find in a jar of salt water to kill them. These pests often come out in the cool of an evening, and can be spotted by torch light. Alternatively, sprinkle slug pellets sparingly round plants and seedlings at risk of attack, or sink containers filled with milk or old beer into the soil almost to their rims to catch slugs.

Caterpillar Large holes appearing in leaves may be caused by caterpillars. Search them out, and destroy!

△ **HANG PHERMONE TRAPS** *in apple trees to attract and catch male codling moth. Phermone traps lure moths to their death, preventing them from fertilising females, so reducing pest attack.*

CHOOSING THE BEST PLANT FOOD

❖

Visit any garden centre and you will be faced with a vast array of fertilizers and plant foods, so how do you choose the right one? To start with, remember that plants need three main foods to grow and flourish. These are nitrogen, phosphorous and potassium, often referred to on the side of the packet as NPK. A number next to each letter indicates their respective proportions in the fertilizer. Nitrogen is needed for leaves and vigorous growth, phosphorous for root development, and potassium for the formation of flowers and fruits.

Consider what you want from each plant, and then choose a fertilizer offering the best balanced diet. For instance, for luscious lawn growth in spring and summer you should choose a food high in nitrogen, but when it comes to flowering pot plants or fruit bushes, plants will need plenty of potassium, or potash. To make life easier, many manufacturers have formulated fertilizers for specific uses, like lawns, shrubs, ericaceous plants, tomatoes and so on. Always use them at exactly the rate described on the packet.

Bonemeal

Growmore

Pellets of poultry manure

❑ Pinch out side shoots of sweet peas being grown as cordons.

❑ Pick off the dead flowerheads from rhododendrons and azaleas.

❑ Sow seed of wallflowers in a corner of the garden to transplant in autumn, planting them with bulbs for flowers next spring.

❑ Support gladioli in exposed gardens by tying their foliage and the developing flower spikes loosely to canes inserted alongside each plant.

❑ Hoe or hand-weed paths and borders regularly. Treat perennial weeds with a systemic weedkiller.

❑ Mark the position of spring-flowering bulbs when their foliage dies down or is removed, so that they will not be damaged by careless digging.

❑ Save any rain that falls in water butts to use on the garden. Give extra water to plants growing at the base of walls where the soil can remain very dry despite rain.

❑ Cut overgrown Clematis alpina and C. macropetala back hard once flowering is over.

❑ Cut down early-flowering perennials like delphiniums, lupins and nepeta to tidy the plants and hopefully encourage a second flush of bloom later in the year.

❑ Pinch out the tips of trailing plants in hanging baskets to make them branch out. Pick off dead flowers every few days.

29

Midsummer – JULY

At the height of summer, when garden displays reach a crescendo, take time to learn from your own successes and from those of friends and neighbours. Consider dead-heading and watering as pleasurable routines to be savoured, in order to prolong the flowering season, but look ahead to preparations for the seasons to come.

△ SWEETPEAS will flower throughout summer if picked regularly. Any left on the plant soon set seed, so pick off dead flowers and pods.

THE FLOWER GARDEN

Bedding plants Dead-head plants in baskets, containers and borders every few days to keep them tidy and productive. Allowing them to set seed looks messy and results in an early end to your flower display.

Autumn-flowering bulbs Buy bulbs to plant now for autumn blooms. These include colchicums, autumn crocus, sternbergia, *Nerine bowdenii* and *Amaryllis belladonna*.

Sweet peas Remember to water regularly if weather is dry, and tie in shoots to their supports to help them climb. Pick or deadhead regularly.

Heathers Spread a fresh mulch of compost or bark round heathers.

Philadelphus When flowering is over, prune out a proportion of the oldest and weakest shoots and prune to improve the shape of the shrubs.

Dahlias Support new growth, which can be easily damaged in strong winds, and feed with a liquid fertilizer.

Blue hydrangeas Water regularly with a solution of colourant to ensure blue varieties remain blue next season, and to encourage pink ones to turn blue where soil conditions are not naturally acid.

Iris Finish splitting congested clumps of bearded iris.

Roses Trim back stems that have finished flowering to a point just above a leaf. This encourages the formation of new growth which carries a late flush of bloom. However, do not prune back varieties that form colourful autumn hips.

30

ROSE SUCKERS

❖

Keep an eye out for rose suckers growing on rootstocks from below ground level. Excavate the soil to find the point of origin and pull cleanly away; suckers can re-grow if simply cut off with secateurs. Cut any suckers growing on the stems of standard roses neatly away with a knife. Avoid hoeing too deeply round roses as damage to the roots encourages suckers to form.

◁ FLAG IRIS should be lifted and divided immediately after flowering. Cut away healthy portions of rhizome, each with a flag of leaves. Replant into prepared soil in an open sunny site.

RAISING NEW LILIES

❖

Propagate new lilies from scales now, carefully lifting bulbs after flowering and removing a few healthy plump outer scales before replanting. Wash in a fungicide solution before placing in clear polythene bags of moist vermiculite to develop. When roots and small bulbs can be seen on each scale, pot up individually and place in a cold frame to grow on for a year before planting in a nursery bed. It will take about three years for bulbs to reach flowering size. Some varieties develop bulbils at each leaf up their stem. When these are plump and come away easily in your hand they can be picked off and planted shallowly in pots or seed trays like large seeds to grow on.

◁ ENCOURAGE A SECOND FLUSH *of roses later in summer by deadheading rose bushes as soon as petals start to fall. Keep an eye out for disease, and spray at the first sign of attack.*

feed established wisteria with a high-potash liquid feed at regular intervals to promote flowering. Always buy a named variety of wisteria, never an un-named seedling. Plants can take several years to establish and flower.

31

Propagating plants

Cuttings Propagate a wide range of tender perennials from cuttings now, including argyranthemums, coleus, osteospermum, fuchsia, pelargonium and felicia. Root into small pots, or strike several cuttings to a larger pot and divide once rooted. These will produce well-rooted young plants in 7.5cm (3in) pots to keep through the winter.

Layering Bend shoots of honeysuckle,

Pruning wisteria Tie in long shoots of new growth to continue developing wisteria's framework. Take the main growth upwards, then along wires so that the flowers can drape from these in tiers. In midsummer, prune back all side shoots to about 15–10cm (6–8in) of the main stem. These same shoots will be shortened still further in winter to about 5cm (2in). This twice-yearly pruning encourages flowering spurs to form along the main shoots.

Care of wisteria Keep well watered during any dry periods in summer and

wisteria or passion flower down to the ground, slit the stem, dust with rooting powder and bury this portion of the stem in the soil. Hold in place with a large stone and do not let the soil dry out. Tie the shoot tip to a cane. Layered shoots take about a year to root well.

Shrubs Take soft and semi-ripe cuttings using non-flowering shoots of shrubs such as cotinus, potentilla, ivy, hydrangea, spiraea, rosemary, weigela, pyracantha, hypericum, honeysuckle, philadelphus, cotoneaster and ceanothus as well as hedging plants.

Roses Many varieties grow easily from shoot cuttings. Produce cuttings about 30cm (12in) long by trimming below a leaf joint at the base, removing lower leaves, and trimming above a leaf at the top to remove the soft shoot tip. Insert to about half their depth in slits in the soil, and leave to root and develop until

the following autumn when you can lift and transplant them.

Carnations To raise new plants, layer non-flowering side shoots. First improve the soil with compost, then bend shoots down to the soil. Make a small diagonal slit through a joint, peg down to hold firmly in place, cover with compost and water in. Keep moist until rooted, when a young plant can be dug up, detached from the parent and planted out.

Camellias Take cuttings of new shoots of camellias, rooting them in gritty compost in a covered propagator.

Hibiscus Pull off non-flowering side shoots with a heel of bark. Trim with a knife and insert into pots of free-draining compost. Place in a shaded frame to root.

Blackberry Bend the tips of new shoots down to soil level and bury in pots of compost. These can be tip-layered to root and form new plants.

THE KITCHEN GARDEN
Vegetable crops

Lettuce Pick while young and tender, cutting every alternate one in a row to leave others more space to develop. Sow weekly to ensure continuity of harvest.

Endive Sow now for autumn crops.

Runner beans Never let plants go short of water. Pick over several times a week to ensure no beans are left to get tough.

Potatoes Dig up second earlies when their tops start to die, but keep maincrop varieties watered, spraying with fungicide to prevent blight.

Brassicas Transplant cabbage, Brussels sprouts and other brassicas from seed beds to their final position and spacing.

Onions Hoe between rows to remove weeds. Keep well watered. Harvest Japanese onions planted last autumn.

Shallots Lift shallots when ripe, laying them on the soil surface to dry before cleaning for storage.

Swedes A final sowing can still be made this month. Cover rows with fleece to protect from flea beetle.

Parsley Sow a row now to produce leaves for picking during the autumn.

Leeks Plant out leeks raised from seed once they are the thickness of a pencil.

Crops to sow This month sow lettuce, spinach, beetroot, radish, endive, spring cabbage, kohl rabi, peas, turnips, chard, salad leaves and Chinese cabbage.

Fruit crops

Strawberries Trim off the foliage to just above the crowns after fruiting, and remove unwanted runners. Rake away old straw.

◁ **FOR ORNAMENTAL EFFECT** *combine flowers and colourful crops to create an attractive potager.*

◁ **PICK STRAWBERRIES** *as they ripen, checking over plants every other day. Cover with netting to prevent birds reaching fruits.*

Figs Shorten the laterals on established figs to just five leaves.

Raspberries Continue thinning out crowded new canes, pruning unwanted canes down to soil level to leave the remaining ones about 15cm (6in) apart. Cover rows of summer-fruiting raspberries with netting to keep the birds away. Pick fruits regularly to enjoy them at their best.

Apples Thin out heavy crops, picking off small, damaged or infected fruits to give the remaining ones more room to develop. Aim to leave fruits spaced about every 10–15cm (4–6in) along the branches.

Cane fruit Once you have picked crops of loganberries, Tayberries and other cane fruits, cut their old fruited canes to the ground. Tie in all the new canes that have formed this year to support wires, spreading them out evenly.

Plums Thin out very heavy crops or support heavily laden branches with props to prevent them breaking under the weight of the crop.

33

PRUNING APPLES AND PEARS
❖

While winter pruning helps control the size, vigour and shape of fruit trees, pruning from mid- to late summer encourages the development of fruiting spurs along the branches. The flowers that will open next spring start forming within buds later this summer, so shorten all side shoots on apple and pear trees to just five leaves, or about 15cm (6in), from their base. Trim any shoots developing from these back to just one leaf, or about 2.5cm (1in). This is particularly important on trained forms of fruit tree, such as those growing as fans, cordons and espaliers, to maintain both their shape and their productivity. Leave shoot tips unpruned to extend the framework of the tree.

LAWN CARE

Mowing Cut every week, or more often if you have time. Collect grass cuttings, mixing them with other material on the compost heap, or use them as a mulch round fruit trees.

Feeding Feed pale lawns with a high-nitrogen liquid feed to green up the leaves and boost growth. If other lawn problems exist, consider applying a triple-action lawn feed, weed and mosskiller instead.

Watering Keep lawns watered during dry spells, recycling washing up and

▷ **TOP UP THE** *water level of ponds weekly in summer. If you see fish gasping at the surface in hot weather, this indicates oxygen shortage. Spray the water surface with a fine shower from the hose as this gets air into the water fast.*

bath water on the lawn. If water is in short supply, and drought threatens, leave the grass longer as it will cope better with periods of water shortage.

Edging Trim edges after mowing. Cut a new edge if they get worn or damaged.

Spiking Spike heavily compacted areas with a fork to relieve compaction.

POND CARE

Blanket weed Remove the long strands of blanket weed that invade ponds in summer by pushing a long stick into the water and twisting it out.

Topping up As water evaporates during the summer, top up the level of ponds and water features with a hosepipe.

Filters Clean pump filters regularly to ensure they do not get clogged up with algae. Install an ultra-violet unit in the pipework to the pump to kill water-borne algae as they pass through.

Pruning Selectively cut away leaves or shoots from very vigorous water lilies and aquatic plants to prevent them smothering their neighbours. Dead-head bog plants and pick off any damaged leaves to stop debris falling into the water.

IN THE GREENHOUSE

Ventilation Open doors and vents daily or control by fitting automatic vent openers. Re-apply shading paint to help reduce high temperatures.

Cuttings Continue taking cuttings of hydrangeas and other plants. Pot up any rooted cuttings taken earlier.

Tomatoes Remove side shoots and tie

CUTTING HEDGES

❖

Most hedges need only a single cut in mid- to late summer. If you time it right, any new growth forming will produce a neat-looking hedge for the winter. Hedges to prune over the coming weeks include beech, hornbeam, thorns like hawthorn, and conifers such as thuja and Lawson cypress. Yew can be cut a little later. All the above plants should be cut with shears or hedge trimmers. The exception is laurel, whose shoots are best cut individually with secateurs to prevent leaving unsightly large, torn leaves which die back.

More regular trimming is required to keep some formal hedges and topiary looking neat and pristine. Box, privet and *Lonicera nitida* need cutting more often, from late spring onwards, to maintain a well-shaped formal hedge. Give the final cut in late summer so that further growth ripens and hardens before the onset of cold weather.

To ensure a level top and an even cut, run a length of string between two canes at either end of the hedge, joined by a string set at the desired height: use this as a guideline to cut up to. With tall

hedges, taper the sides slightly as you cut, leaving the base a little wider than the top to allow more light to reach the hedge. Spread a large sheet along the base of the hedge to collect prunings, then shred and compost them.

main stems to supports. Pick ripe fruits as they form and remove leaves below the lowest truss to improve the air circulation. Check watering daily, as intermittent watering can result in split fruit. Feed every week.

Cucumbers Harvest fruits regularly. Continue pinching off the tips of side shoots two leaves beyond a female flowers. Remove male flowers.

△ **PICKING AUBERGINE** *fruits once they have swollen to reach their full size. Regular picking encourages further flowers to form.*

Melons Pollinate female flowers, easily identified by a swelling behind the bloom, by dabbing with pollen from a male bloom. Support developing fruits in small nets attached to the greenhouse frame to hold their weight.

MIDSUMMER CHECKLIST

❑ When water is scarce at the height of summer, give priority to soft fruits and vegetables, where watering can significantly increase your yields.

❑ Never let hanging baskets and containers go short of water; add a high-potash liquid feed to the water every week.

❑ Consider setting up an automated system connected to the tap to make watering easier, enabling you to control the time and duration of irrigation with a computerized tap timer.

❑ Keep on top of both annual and perennial weeds. Regularly hand-weed borders and hoe the soil between plants during dry weather to create a dust mulch.

❑ Apply mulches of compost over the soil to prevent the germination of annual weed seedlings. Use contact or non-residual weedkillers only if all other methods of weed control have failed.

❑ Wipe aphids off leaves by hand or use soap-based sprays.

❑ Pick fresh herbs regularly to dry or to freeze.

❑ Visit rose nurseries to see new varieties in bloom, and order now for autumn delivery and planting.

❑ Compost all your kitchen and garden waste, mixing shredded prunings and other material with lawn cuttings. Add an activator to boost decomposition.

35

PEST CONTROL UNDER GLASS

❖

- Examine plants each week for signs of pests, picking them off or treating at once if any are found.

- Introduce the small parasitic wasp, Encarsia formosa, to the greenhouse if whitefly are present. Refrain from using any chemicals either before or after their introduction or these beneficial predators may be killed by chemical residues.

- Damp down greenhouse floors each morning or mist lightly over plants to increase humidity which deters red spider mite attack. If infestation is getting severe, introduce the predatory mite Phytoseiulus persimilis.

- Water pots of compost with a solution of nematodes for the control of vine weevil grubs.

Late Summer – AUGUST

It is a good idea to simply relax this month, although so many plants are looking their best and vying for your attention with both colour and fragrance. Enjoy the simple pleasure of pottering in the late-summer garden, with pruners to hand for regular dead-heading to keep the display looking its very best. Look to the future by taking choice cuttings.

36

THE FLOWER GARDEN

Bulbs Plant out bulbs of colchicums, sternbergia, autumn crocus and the Madonna lily (*Lilium candidum*).

Perennials Cut off the old flower spikes of early-flowered perennials, like delphiniums, polemoniums, lupins and foxtail lilies (*Eremurus*).

Everlasting flowers Pick dried flowerheads and seedheads from a range of plants. Annuals like limonium and helichrysum are at their best, as are seedheads of poppies, nigella, lunaria, moluccella, eryngiums and a range of grasses. Hang upside down in bunches in a dry, airy room.

Supports Late-flowering perennials like chrysanthemums and Michaelmas daisies are growing taller by the day and getting more top-heavy as their flowers develop. Check plant supports are in place, adding more canes and string to ensure they hold up and cannot be flattened by wind and rain.

Hedges Trim back laurel hedges using secateurs to remove complete shoots. Also cut privet, beech, hornbeam, yew, box and holly. Most conifer hedges can be given their single cut of the year at the end of this month.

Sweet peas Untie the stems of cordon-trained sweet peas which have reached the tops of their supports. Lower stems to the ground and re-tie the tips to provide new canes for them to climb.

Dahlias Pick dahlias regularly and continue tying in stems to their supports. Maintain regular liquid feeding. Trap earwigs that can damage flower buds, especially on dahlias, in upturned pots full of straw or crumpled newspaper on top of short canes. Empty out daily and destroy earwigs.

Camellias Camellias will be forming flower buds now to bloom next spring, so ensure they never go short of water or their buds can drop prematurely.

Roses Prune rambler roses when their flowering is over.

THE KITCHEN GARDEN
Vegetable crops

Harvesting Pick crops regularly to keep plants productive, particularly on courgettes and beans. Pick sweet corn while cobs are sweet and tender. Raise large marrows selected for storage up onto bricks to keep in the sun to ripen and harden their skins.

Watering Water crops as regularly as possible to increase yields, especially runner beans and others carrying fruits and pods. Maincrop potato yields will increase considerably if watered now.

Celery Never allow celery to get dry

◁ **KEEP BORDERS BLOOMING** *by watering well at least once a week during dry weather. Include a high potash liquid feed at the same time, and cut down any faded flower spikes.*

HOME COMPOSTING

❖

Virtually all garden waste can be recycled into compost, along with old vegetables, fruit, peelings and egg shells from the kitchen. If possible, invest in two compost heaps, so that while one is rotting down fresh material can be added to the other. A totally enclosed bin with a lid is far better than an open one with slatted sides. Aim to mix together a variety of materials as they are added to the heap. Avoid putting in thick layers of lawn mowings, for instance, which can form a soggy mass. Add a little at a time between layers of clippings and other waste. Shred thick and woody material before composting. Mix a biological compost activator into the heap to speed up the composting process, and make sure the material never dries out.

△ **COVER COMPOST BINS** *with a solid lid or simply a sheet of polythene to prevent rain soaking contents, and retain the heat generated during composting.*

FRUIT PRUNING

❖

- Finish summer pruning apple trees by cutting back all side shoots.

- Remove old fruited canes of summer raspberries completely, cutting them off at soil level. Tie in and space out the remaining canes of new growth, which will fruit next summer.

- Give old blackcurrant bushes their annual prune, removing about a quarter of the oldest branches to make room for new growth.

- Prune out shoots of peaches and nectarines that carried fruit. Train in the new shoots to their supports, pinching off any side shoots growing.

△ **PRUNE GOOSEBERRIES** *by shortening all side shoots back to five leaves. Also remove any shoots badly damaged by mildew.*

at the root. Keep watered and earth up trench varieties to blanch their stems.
Tomatoes Pinch out the tops of outdoor tomatoes, as any further flowers developing now will not form ripe fruit before autumn.
Blanching Cover a few endive plants with plates to blanch their leaves.
Sowing Sow hardy varieties of winter lettuce outside or in frames. Sow winter spinach. Enjoy tasty turnip tops this autumn by sowing a few now.
Ordering Order onion sets and garlic for autumn planting.

Fruit crops

Strawberries Tidy up strawberry beds, cutting off unwanted runners, and trimming all the foliage down to the crown with shears. Transplant strawberry runners rooted in pots or plant up new beds with healthy plants obtained from a specialist grower.
Tree fruits Water apples, pears and other fruits to help increase their size. Pick early-ripening apple varieties like 'Redsleeves', 'Discovery', 'Epicure' and 'George Cave' which can be eaten straight from the tree.
Bird protection Cover cherries and autumn-fruiting raspberries and blackberries with nets, or hang reflective scarers in trees to keep birds away.
Plums Once fruit has been picked, prune back side shoots to three leaves, and cut out dead wood. Do not prune shoots needed to extend the framework.

LAWN CARE

Mowing Continue regular mowing to keep lawns looking smart, and trim the edges each week.
Spiking Spike lawns with a hollow-tined aerator, sweeping up the soil cores left on the lawn surface. Brush sand or gritty compost into the holes.
Repairs Repair damaged lawn edges, and patch up worn areas. Spot-treat individual weeds with a herbicide or dig out by hand.
New lawns Prepare sites for sowing or laying lawns in early autumn.

◁ **PICK DAMSONS**, *plums and gages, allowing them to fully ripen on the tree for the best flavour. Hang bird scarers among branches to reduce damage, and try to keep wasps away.*

△ **DAMP DOWN** *the greenhouse floor each morning to increase humidity. This helps reduce the temperature and prevent red spider mite.*

IN THE GREENHOUSE

Watering Keep crops in pots and grow bags, like tomatoes, peppers and cucumbers, well watered. Never allow their compost to get dry; feed weekly.

Keeping cool Ventilate daily to keep temperatures down, opening doors in addition to roof and side vents. Close on cool nights.

Propagation Take cuttings of tender perennials like fuchsias, pelargoniums and argyranthemums now, to produce well-rooted plants that will survive the winter. Pot up the rooted cuttings.

Cyclamen Sow cyclamen seed to raise indoor flowering pot plants. Water dormant plants at the end of this month to bring them back into growth.

Gloxinias Reduce watering of gloxinias when they have finished flowering. Once their foliage has dried, pick off and store tubers for the winter.

Hyacinth Plant prepared bulbs in bowls, keeping to one variety per bowl to ensure they flower uniformly.

Bulbs Plant freesia, lachenalia and early indoor daffodils, like 'Paperwhite'.

LATE-SUMMER CHECKLIST

❐ Collect seed from a range of flowers. Some can be saved and stored for future use and others, like foxgloves and aquilegia, sown freshly by scattering around to fill gaps in borders.

❐ Pot up a few clumps of parsley and chives, cutting off their leaves to encourage fresh growth for winter use.

❐ Water pots of nerines to encourage growth and autumn flowering.

❐ Regularly dead-head flowers in hanging baskets and tubs.

❐ Order spring-flowering bulbs for autumn planting.

❐ Pick fresh herbs to dry or chop and store in ice cubes in the freezer.

❐ Sow hardy annual flowers in pots now to flower early next year.

❐ Remove suckers developing from the roots of roses and other fruiting and ornamental trees.

❐ Prune lavender bushes if this was not completed last season.

❐ Tie stems of late flowering chrysanthemums to supports.

❐ Take leaf cuttings from African violets, streptocarpus, *Begonia rex* and other foliage pot plants.

❐ Pinch out the shoot tips of wallflowers to encourage branching.

❐ Cut down the tops of potatoes if they show signs of blight attack.

39

Early Autumn – SEPTEMBER

After a relaxing summer it is time for a new surge of activity in the autumn garden. It is an exciting time because, as we finish collecting the produce and clearing away the remains of one season, we start putting plans in place for the next. The first bulbs can already be planted to flower next spring.

△ FOR A GOOD *display in pots, plant two layers of bulbs, one below the other. In a big container, you could add a third tier, their tips at soil level.*

THE FLOWER GARDEN

Tender perennials Lift plants from summer bedding displays, clean off dead flowers and leaves, then pot them up and bring into the greenhouse or home for the winter.

Sweet peas Sow seed in pots in autumn, and overwinter plants in a cold frame to plant out next spring. These plants will flower earlier than those sown outdoors in spring.

Moving shrubs Overgrown or badly positioned shrubs and conifers can be transplanted to a better site now. Thoroughly prepare the new planting site, digging compost deeply into the soil. Very large shrubs could lose quite a lot of roots during the process, so prune out some of the oldest top growth to help them survive.

Rose care Finish pruning out all shoots from rambler and climbing roses that carried flowers as soon as they have faded. Remove suckers from round bush roses, or any growing from the stems of standards.

Pruning perennials Cut down faded and dying flower stems from border perennials, tidying up the plants but leave as much foliage as possible. Collect, wash and store away plant supports no longer needed.

Dahlias Tie tall flower stems to supports the prevent wind damage.

Continue cutting blooms for the home.

Hardy annuals In mild regions hardy annuals can be sown outside in autumn instead of delaying until spring. Sow where you would like them to flower. Varieties to choose include calendula, nigella, godetia, eschscholzia, larkspur, candytuft, annual alyssum, Shirley poppies, scabious and limnanthes.

Anemones Plant tubers of anemone 'De Caen' and 'Saint Brigid' at intervals to extend their flowering next spring.

Dutch iris To follow on from spring bulbs, plant blocks of Dutch iris in sunny positions, setting them about 7.5cm (3in) deep by 15cm (6in) apart. These flower in early summer.

New planting Early autumn is a good time to plant evergreen shrubs, conifers

40

▽ EVEN LARGE RHODODENDRONS *move surprisingly well since they have a shallow root system. If you have time, prepare the plant a year in advance to encourage it to grow lots of new, fibrous roots into a compost-rich trench.*

△ **THE LATE DISPLAY** *of dahlias will continue right up to the first frost if plants are regularly deadheaded. Once foliage is blackened by frost, tubers can be lifted, cleaned and stored for winter.*

SPRING BEDDING

Clear areas of summer bedding now getting past its best to make room for spring bedding, which can be planted out as soon as space becomes available. All old plant remains can be lifted, chopped up and composted. Early planting allows the bedding to settle, establish new roots, and develop bushy plants before the onset of winter. For best effect, base your spring displays on a single colour theme, choosing varieties which flower for a long period. These could include wallflowers, pansies, sweet Williams, primulas, polyanthus, forget-me-nots and others. To add a second tier of colour, and extend the flowering season still further; underplant bedding with taller tulips to grow up through them in matching or contrasting colours.

or hedging plants, like laurel. Warm soil conditions encourage root growth and establishment before winter.

Carnations Side shoots layered to the soil in summer should now have rooted, and can be detached from the parent and planted in a new site. Alternatively, lift and pot up into 10cm (4in) pots.

Keep in a frame over winter, and plant outside in borders next spring.

THE KITCHEN GARDEN
Vegetable crops

Onions Lift onion crops now, easing each bulb up with a fork to break its roots, then leaving to dry on the soil surface for a day before collecting. Lay in the greenhouse to dry fully before cleaning and storing in a shed or garage.

Watering Continue watering outdoor crops like tomato, beans and courgettes to encourage more fruits and pods to form and ripen.

Spring cabbage Plant out at close spacing. From early spring, harvest every other cabbage, leaving more space for the remaining ones to develop. Plant in shallow trenches so that soil can be pulled up round the stems for extra support as they grow.

Lettuce Sow hardy winter varieties of lettuce under cloches or in the borders of a greenhouse.

Celery Continue wrapping trench varieties of celery with newspaper or cardboard, then draw earth up round the stems to blanch them ready for

41

BUYING AND PLANTING BULBS

A wide range of spring-flowering bulbs can be planted now, including crocus, hyacinth, muscari, iris and daffodil. Most should be planted directly in borders where you would like them to flower. Extend the season of interest of your winter patio tubs into spring by the addition of bulbs, as well as planting bulbs, especially fragrant varieties, in pots and bowls for indoor displays. Choose bulbs which look healthy, with no signs of rot or mould, and which are firm to the touch. Bulbs are graded by size, larger bulbs costing more but producing better blooms. As a general rule, plant so that bulbs are covered by at least twice their depth in soil. Most garden centres sell only a limited range of bulbs, but a greater variety is available by mail-order.

WINTER POTS AND BASKETS

Empty tubs, baskets and window boxes of summer bedding past their best, and replant to provide winter interest. Include a balance of hardy shrubs along with a few winter- and spring-flowering bedding plants and dwarf bulbs. Good shrubs include winter-flowering heathers, variegated euonymus, gaultheria and dwarf conifers. Cover the edges with trailing ivies, which can be pegged to the sides of baskets for complete cover. Be generous when planting to produce an instant, mature look. Water well and then check regularly, at least twice a week. Winter pots will not require weekly feeding, but occasional liquid feeds in late winter and early spring will boost growth. Raise tubs off the ground on bricks to improve drainage.

▷ **FLOPPING ONION FOLIAGE** *is a sure sign that onions are readey to harvest. Ease each bulb up gently with a fork to break its roots, then lie on the soil to dry and ripen in the sun.*

cutting in late autumn.

Turnip tops Make a sowing of turnips now for cutting as green turnip tops later in the year.

Potatoes Keep the foliage of maincrop varieties free from potato blight disease until ready to harvest, using regular fungicide sprays. If blight appears, cut all the foliage off right away to prevent the disease spreading to the tubers. Continue harvesting early varieties as required for the kitchen.

Outdoor tomatoes Strip off both ripe and unripe fruits from outdoor plants before they are damaged by an early frost or blight. Alternatively, lift the entire plants and hang them in the greenhouse for the remaining fruits to ripen under cover.

Root crops Carefully lift maincrop carrots and beetroot before autumn rain causes the roots to swell and split. Cut off the foliage and store healthy crops in boxes between layers of almost dry sand or compost. These keep in good condition for several months under frost-free conditions.

Endive Cover a few plants each week with plates to blanch them for use in salads. Complete blanching takes about two weeks. Upturned flower pots can also be used, but cover holes

◁ **A BOX SPIRAL** *provides year-round structure. Because its growth is slow compared to privet, one or two clips a growing season will suffice. Keep slopes parallel, like a living helter-skelter.*

with a tile to exclude light. Take precautions against slugs and snails.

Leeks Continue blanching leeks, covering the stem of plants with tubes of cardboard or drainpipe. Light must be excluded from the base of the stem to ensure good blanching.

Harvesting Pick crops at their best including marrows, runner beans, ridge cucumbers, spinach, sweet corn, radish, beetroot and salads. In cold districts complete harvesting before the end of this season.

Fruit crops

Strawberries Well-rooted runners in pots can be planted out to form new beds. Healthy certified new stock should also be available to buy. Water well until established. Clear up strawberry beds, removing unwanted runners and hoeing between rows to remove any weeds.

Peaches Continue pruning to remove all shoots that have carried fruit, then tying in new shoots to replace them.

Apples Harvest early-ripening varieties like 'Discovery', 'Beauty of Bath' and 'Blenheim Orange', and eat while crisp and at their best. These early ripening varieties do not keep well, and cannot be stored.

Cane fruits Prune all old fruited canes from hybrid cane fruits and loganberries at soil level. Tie in the new canes produced this year, spacing them out evenly. These will carry a crop of fruit next summer.

New fruit Order new trees and bushes to plant later this autumn and winter.

Cherries Cut out dead wood from fan-trained cherries. Prune back all side shoots previously shortened in summer to just three buds, and tie in growth to the support canes.

Raising new gooseberries

Propagate new bushes by taking hardwood cuttings from healthy plants before their leaves drop. Take stems of the current season's growth and remove the soft tip to leave a cutting about 25cm (10in) long. Remove all buds except the top three or four, so that the resulting bush has a head of branches on a clean stem. Cover an area of soil with black polythene, pushing the cuttings down through it to about half their depth. Alternatively, insert in slits in the soil with grit in the base, firming soil back round them with your boot.

LAWN CARE

Sowing a new lawn This is an ideal time to sow a new lawn into soil prepared during the previous season. Be sure it has been well firmed and allowed to settle before levelling. Sow evenly, marking out the area and scattering seed in both directions, then raking it into the soil surface. Water the area if it does not rain, and ensure the soil remains moist until germination is complete, within two to three weeks. Use netting or scarers to keep birds away. Refrain from walking over the new lawn. Trim only lightly, with mower blades set high, when the growth is about 4–5cm (1½–2in) long.

Over-sowing Where grass growth is very thin and sparse, over-seed now with a suitable grass seed mixture. Cut the lawn, then rake the surface to remove debris. Sprinkle with seed, sweeping it into the surface. On small areas, cover with a fine layer of compost.

General care Continue regular mowing, raking off dead grass and any debris that has accumulated deep down in the lawn over the summer.

Feeding Apply an autumn lawn food to encourage good root growth and strengthen grass for the winter. However, be sure not to apply a spring feed, which is not suitable at this time.

LAYING TURF

1 *After digging the ground deeply, sprinkle the fertilizer dressing evenly over the soil and rake well in, levelling the ground and removing stones and roots as you go.*

2 *Firm the whole area over, using your feet and allowing the weight to sink through your heels. A roller will only flatten down the peaks and leave the hollows loose.*

3 *To avoid footmarks pitting the surface of the prepared soil, work from a long plank. Start at one edge and work forwards across the area. Unroll the turves and lay them out in a row, with their edges butting tightly together.*

4 *Firm down the first row with the back of a rake. Move the plank on a little and lay the second row of turf like bricks in a wall, so the joints between adjacent turves do not run continuously. Water regularly until established.*

▷ **REPLANT BULBS** *lifted last spring to make room for summer bedding. These can be planted in pots or directly back into borders.*

POND CARE

Plant division Lift and divide large marginal plants, or those growing in bog gardens. Cut up or pull apart, ensuring that each piece being replanted has a portion or root and shoot attached.

Primulas Plant out hardy primulas raised from seed or divisions.

Leaf netting Get ready to cover pools with netting to keep out fallen leaves.

IN THE GREENHOUSE

Cyclamen Sparingly water potted cyclamen that were dried off for the summer to encourage them back into growth. Pick off early flowers to ensure a good display later.

Freesias Plant pots of prepared freesia corms to use for displays or cut flowers.

Lachenalia Bulbs should be available for planting in pots now. Any saved from last year can be knocked out of their old containers and repotted in fresh compost.

Cuttings This is your last chance to take cuttings of geraniums and fuchsias which will root well in small pots to be kept through winter. Continue taking cuttings from impatiens, coleus, tradescantia, heliotrope, African violets, begonias and other plants.

Hardy annuals Sow pots of hardy annuals, like calendula and zinnia, for colourful displays in cold greenhouses and porches.

Clean-up Once old crops in pots and growing bags are past their best, pick any remaining produce. Cut down plants and take all the debris to the compost heap.

Cleaning glass Wash shade paints from the outside of the glazing, and clean all glass thoroughly inside and out to remove dirt and algal growth. This ensures maximum penetration of light during winter.

Heaters Make sure greenhouse heaters are in good working order, and paraffin or bottled gas supplies in stock.

Bulbs in bowls Plant early-flowering bulbs, including prepared hyacinths, in pots or bowls. Use bulb fibre or seed

44

◁ **TO MAKE** *a softwood cutting, cut 10cm (4in) from the tip of a young shoot, remove the leaves from the bottom half of the shoot and cut off cleanly just below a leaf joint, and remove flowers and buds. Dip the cut end in hormone rooting powder, then push each cutting into a pot of seed compost and water in.*

compost, planting so that the tips of the bulbs lie at the surface. After watering, place in a cool, sheltered position·for the bulbs to root. Bring indoors only when shoots have developed to about 5–7.5cm (2–3in) long.

Begonias Reduce watering and allow the top growth on begonias and gloxinias to die down.

Achimenes Lay pots of hot water plant on their side so that the foliage will die down and compost dry out. Rhizomes can be left in the dry compost for the winter, or tipped out, cleaned and stored in envelopes.

Watering As nights get cooler and plant growth slows down in autumn, gradually reduce the quantity and frequency of watering. Allow compost to almost dry out between waterings, and stand pots on greenhouse staging instead of on moist capillary matting.

Chrysanthemums Bring late flowering varieties in pots into the greenhouse in case flower buds get damaged by frost.

Potting Complete potting up plants or cuttings early in the month to ensure plants get established before winter.

Cutting the cost of greenhouse heating

Insulation Line the inside of your greenhouse with bubble polythene to double glaze it and reduce heat loss. Also hang a curtain of polythene across the doorway to reduce draughts. Use thick sheets of white polystyrene to line the walls along the north side, especially under the staging.

Sealing draughts Mend poorly fitting doors and vents, sealing over low-level vents completely with clear polythene during winter to reduce cold draughts.

Broken glass Replace cracked panes which not only let in cold, but can be dangerous.

Storage heaters Place dustbins filled with water under greenhouse staging to act as storage heaters. These warm up during the day, releasing their heat at night. This warm water can be used for watering plants.

Heated benches Instead of heating the whole house in winter, install an electrically heated bench to keep plants on, covered by a tent of bubble polythene to keep out the cold.

COLLECTING LEAVES

All autumn leaves can be collected and composted into leafmould for use as a mulch, a soil conditioner or for mixing with potting compost. Garden vacuums are useful for collecting leaves, and some models shred them as they collect, speeding up their decomposition. On lawns, use a rotary lawn mower with blades set high to gather and shred leaves. Small quantities can be mixed with other garden waste and put on the compost heap, but large quantities of leaves are best stacked in leaf bins, or kept in black plastic sacks, with their tops tied, and a few air holes punched in the sides. Add a leaf compost activator to speed up decomposition, which should take from 6–12 months, depending on the type of leaf.

EARLY-AUTUMN CHECKLIST

❑ Cut down border perennials now past their best.

❑ Collect up, clean and store away canes and plant supports.

❑ Dig up and compost old summer bedding plants.

❑ Be ready to net ponds to prevent autumn leaves blowing in.

❑ Cut down any marginal plants round pools that are dying back.

❑ Plant spring-flowering bulbs in pots and containers.

❑ Dig up bulbs and corms of non-hardy varieties to store in a dry and frost-free place over winter. Packing them in dry compost helps insulate them and prevents dehydration.

❑ Lift gladioli corms carefully, keeping named varieties separate. Cut foliage down to within 2.5cm (1in) of the corm, clean off any soil and pick off small cormlets to store separately in envelopes.

❑ Lift and dry begonia tubers and bulbs of canna lilies and eucomis and treat in a similar way.

❑ Plant lilies as soon as bulbs are available.

45

◁ SAVING SEED *from garden plants is an excellent method of building up stocks, and helps you share favourite plants with friends.*

Mid-Autumn – OCTOBER

Autumn colours transform the garden, changing almost daily as the foliage on deciduous trees and shrubs puts on a final show before falling. With bulb planting yet to be completed and the end-of-season clear-up in progress, there is still plenty to keep the gardener busy this month. Autumn colours transform the garden, changing almost daily as the foliage on deciduous trees and shrubs puts on a final show before falling.

△ **TO NATURALIZE**
crocus bulbs in the lawn, strip back a piece of turf, scatter the corms and plant them where they fall, then simply replace the turf over them.

THE FLOWER GARDEN

Sweet peas Sow in deep containers in cold frames. Sow several per pot and either thin to leave the strongest or leave to plant out in groups.

Tulips Plant bulbs this month, setting them up to 15–20cm (6–8in) deep where you want them to naturalize.

Spring bedding Plant out wallflowers, forget-me-nots, primulas, polyanthus, bellis, pansies and other bedding plants for spring flower displays. Many can be interplanted with spring bulbs which will grow up among them.

Planting This is a good time to plant shrubs, conifers and hedging. Soil conditions are still warm, so roots will grow to get plants established before the onset of winter.

Dahlias Lift tubers as soon as the foliage has been blackened by frost. Clean off soil, cut back stems, and stand upside down to drain water from them. Label, then store in boxes of compost.

Rambler roses Finish pruning as soon as possible, removing all old stems.

THE KITCHEN GARDEN
Vegetable crops

Harvesting Finish picking ripened marrows and bring in for winter storage. Pick all remaining outdoor tomatoes and tender crops. Lift potatoes, clean them and store in paper sacks in a frost-free place. Lift carrots and beetroot and store in boxes of compost.

Peas Sow a row of hardy peas and cover with cloches. Broad beans can also be sown now.

Brussels sprouts Pick off yellowing leaves and harvest when large enough.

◁ **LATE FLOWERING** *bulbs, like* Nerine bowdenii, *are equally at home in a warm, sunny site or in pots of free-draining compost.*

46

FLOWER BORDER CARE

- Cut down all dead flower stems on herbaceous perennials, and tidy borders to remove foliage and plant remains; compost this material. Leave late-flowering perennials.

- Divide congested perennials and herbs, like bergamot and lady's mantle, from mid- to late autumn, or delay until spring.

- Collect plant supports and canes to store for winter.

- Fork over the soil between plants in established borders to loosen the surface; remove weeds, then spread on a layer of well-rotted compost.

◁ TO KEEP BORDER DISPLAYS *going well into autumn, include a selection of asters for late flower colour. Although hydrangeas are now past their best, their flower heads change with the seasons. Cut to use in indoor arrangements.*

Celery Finish earthing up trench celery to blanch the stems.

Asparagus Cut all ferny shoots right down to soil level.

Cauliflowers Bend outer leaves over curds to prevent them discolouring.

Artichokes Finish harvesting globe artichokes before cutting down their tops. Cut back screens of Jerusalem artichokes to about 30cm (12in) from the ground once the leaves turn brown, and dig up the crop as required. Cover with a mulch to protect over winter.

Garlic Plant individual cloves of a hardy variety during autumn, spacing them about 15cm (6in) apart. Choose an open, sunny and free-draining site.

Herbs Pot up parsley, chives and other herbs for winter use, and keep on a

47

sunny windowsill. Plant a few roots of mint in shallow trays and bring into a warm greenhouse to force fresh shoots to use over the coming months.

Digging Remove old crops, clear the ground and dig compost or manure into the soil. Leave heavy soil rough-dug so frost can penetrate to help break it down.

Fruit crops

Cherries Prune out fruited stems from 'Morello' and other varieties.

Cuttings Take hardwood cuttings from healthy bushes of gooseberries and currants, using shoots of the current season's wood.

Blackberries Prune all canes that have carried a crop of fruit back to ground level and tie new shoots produced this year in their place.

Blackcurrants Finish pruning old bushes, removing about a quarter of the oldest branches.

Strawberries Clean and tidy established strawberry beds, removing weeds and any runners growing between rows.

Harvesting and storing Continue to pick apples and pears as each variety ripens. Damaged fruits should be eaten or cooked right away; store only healthy fruits. Check crops in store regularly for signs of deterioration.

Grease bands Wrap grease bands round the trunks of apples, plums and cherries to catch the winter moth as she climbs to lay her eggs.

LAWN CARE

Leaves Collect up leaves as soon as they fall. Wet leaves can smother grass, causing it to discolour, so hoover or rake up regularly.

Raking Rake and scarify lawns with a powered lawn rake to remove thatch and accumulated debris.

Spiking Improve drainage and relieve surface compaction with a hollow-tined aerator. Pick up all the soil cores, then sweep sharp sand or grit down into all the holes. This creates drainage channels over the whole lawn.

Top-dressing Spread a layer of gritty loam-based compost over lawns as a top dressing. This layer should only be very thin, and helps improve the surface soil.

Repairs Build up hollows over several months with thin layers of compost. Also mend any damaged lawn edges.

48

△ **GENTLY CUP PEARS** *and twist slightly as you lift. Ripe fruits should come away easily in your hand. If unsure, leave a little longer.*

▷ **CAREFULLY PICK APPLES** *which will be stored for winter use. Wrap fruits individually in paper, and lie on trays in a cool, airy but frost-free place.*

IN THE GREENHOUSE

Watering Reduce watering now to suit the demands of each plant. It is far better to water individual pots in saucers than to use self-watering benches of capillary matting. Keep the atmosphere as dry as possible.

Protection Bring pots of tender bulbs and perennials into the greenhouse for the winter. Canna lilies, eucomis and many other bulbs die down completely, so require no water over winter.

Cuttings This is your last chance to take cuttings of argyranthemum, penstemon and other perennials.

Chrysanthemums Bring potted late-flowering varieties under glass before frost strikes. Keep the greenhouse well ventilated and check watering each day.

Begonias Refrain from watering tuberous begonias, gloxinias and achimenes to allow foliage to die down.

Fuchsias Reduce watering over winter, but never allow the compost to dry out completely. Wrap pipe insulation round the stems of standard fuchsias.

Old crops Remove old crops and growing bags once pickings diminish.

Young plants Finish potting on rooted cuttings and seedlings. Pinch out the tips of schizanthus and other plants to encourage well-branched, bushy growth.

Heating Get ready to clean glass and fix up bubble insulation. Check that heaters are working efficiently.

POND CARE

Marginals Cut down marginal plants in pools and perennial bog plants as their foliage dies back for the winter.

Netting Stretch large sheets of small meshed netting over ponds to prevent leaves blowing in; anchor it down

△ **BUBBLE INSULATION** *can be fixed to the inside of greenhouses to act as double glazing. This helps reduce heat loss, cut out draughts, and significantly reduce winter heating bills.*

tightly round the edges. On small formal ponds, make a frame covered with netting to fit right over the pond. This can be removed once all leaves have fallen and been collected.

Winter storage Remove pumps and filters from fountains and waterfalls. Clean well before storing indoors.

Heating Float a pond heater on fish ponds, especially those made from concrete, to prevent thick ice forming on the surface. This expands to crack ponds and can trap harmful gases.

PREPARING FOR THE COLD WEATHER
❖

Cooler days and even colder nights signal a timely warning of frost risk. Move all tender plants, especially tender perennials and shrubs like pelargoniums, fuchsias, cordylines and marguerites, to the shelter of a frost-free greenhouse. Lift and pot up those you have enjoyed during the summer in flower borders, and bring under cover as soon as possible.

MID-AUTUMN CHECKLIST

❏ Sprinkle fertilizer over areas to be planted up this autumn.

❏ Move shrubs found to be growing in the wrong place, or to relieve congestion in packed borders.

❏ Empty and wash out water butts, before replacing them to collect winter rain.

❏ Order fruit trees, bushes, roses and shrubs to plant out over winter. Where possible, choose newer, disease-resistant varieties.

❏ Check all tree stakes and ties. Replace loose and damaged ties, and loosen any which are too tight.

❏ Continue taking hardwood cuttings of roses and shrubs like cornus, willow, buddleja and ribes.

❏ Propagate hedging varieties of conifers from cuttings, using shoots of the new growth. Root directly into gritty soil in a cold frame.

❏ Throw a net over a branch carrying holly berries to keep the birds away and keep this to cut for indoor decorations.

❏ Order farmyard manure and compost required for soil conditioning and mulching.

❏ Plant up patio tubs for autumn and winter colour.

❏ Finish planting hyacinth, crocus, dwarf iris and other bulbs in pots which can be brought indoors to flower early next year.

49

Late Autumn – November

There is still much to be done in the autumn garden, with ground to prepare and new shrubs, roses and hedging to plant. After harvesting crops from the kitchen garden, tidy up flower borders and rake up the last leaves to bring autumn to a close, while preparing the garden ready for the next season.

△ IN A SUDDEN *frost, use old newspapers for emergency lagging. Once compost freezes solid, plant roots are unable to take up moisture and even the hardiest plants can die.*

THE FLOWER GARDEN

Agapanthus Move pots to a cold greenhouse or frame for the winter.

Chrysanthemums Once late-flowering varieties have finished blooming they can be dug up, labelled and stored in boxes. They can be encouraged into growth in late winter to form cuttings.

Hedging Plant now for the best value hedges, plant bare-rooted deciduous shrubs like beech and hawthorn.

Buddleja Shorten tall stems by half to reduce wind rock, but wait until spring before pruning back hard.

Jasmine Take heel cuttings of winter jasmine and root in pots in a frame.

Rock gardens Pick off leaves that have fallen on alpine plants, and give a final weed by hand. Replenish gravel mulches round alpines.

Soil preparation When weather allows, dig over and prepare soil for new planting.

Planting Continue planting trees, shrubs, roses, conifers and hedging.

Bulbs Finish planting up tulips

▷ DAZZLING DISPLAYS *of late chrysanthemums add welcome colour to tired borders. These hardy perennials can continue blooming right into winter.*

◁ **PLANT A PRIVET HEDGE** *into well-prepared soil: once in place, a hedge can last many decades and this is the only chance you will have to improve growing conditions. Cut hard back after planting to create a hedge that will be fully clothed with foliage right down to the ground.*

PLANTING ROSES

Bare-rooted roses should be arriving in garden centres or will be available by mail-order. Plant at any time from now until late winter, preparing the soil well, removing weeds and adding plenty of compost and fertilizer. Avoid planting new roses on a site where roses have grown for many years unless fresh soil and compost have been added. In addition to choosing for colour, fragrance and form, choose rose varieties offering good natural resistance to disease.

and other spring-flowering bulbs. Lift dahlias, cannas, gladioli or other tender bulbs for storage under dry and frost-free conditions.

Roses Check stakes and ties on standard roses. Collect and destroy fallen leaves infected with black spot. Shorten long stems and top growth on standard roses to reduce wind rock.

THE KITCHEN GARDEN
Vegetable crops

Peas Sow hardy varieties in well drained soil, covering with cloches for extra protection.

Brussels sprouts Pick crops which are large enough from the bottom of the stem upwards and remove yellowing and fallen leaves.

Bean trench Dig out a trench where next summer's runner bean crop will be grown, and fill the base of it with leaves, compost, old crops, weeds and kitchen waste over the winter. Cover with soil in spring before planting the beans.

Chicory Lift chicory roots, plant in pots, then place in the greenhouse

△ **FLOWER HEADS ON HARDY PERENNIALS** *like sedum and* Phlomis russeliana *can be left in place throughout winter to add structure and form to the borders. Cut down in early spring instead.*

covered with upturned pots to force tasty chicons.

Jerusalem artichokes Cut down the tops and carefully dig out of the soil, cleaning and storing in paper bags in a similar way to potatoes.

Root crops Lift and store beetroot, turnips, salsify and scorzonera in boxes of compost. Parsnips can also be stored, or left in the soil. However, they can be attacked by soil pests, and are difficult to harvest if the ground freezes.

Crops in store Check vegetables in store for signs of rot or deterioration.

DEVELOPING A NEW VEGETABLE PLOT

This is the ideal time to prepare a new plot, digging over the site deeply while adding large quantities of well-rotted compost or manure. Grass can be dug in, turning it upside down in the base of a trench then covering it with soil to prevent re-growth. Plots dug early can be left rough so that the frost and winter weather helps break down large lumps, and birds can forage for soil pests.

52

Fruit crops

New planting Prepare the soil for planting new fruit trees and bushes. Place orders to ensure early delivery to complete planting before next spring.

Supports Check post and wire supports, and replace any which are loose or damaged. Put up new supports ready for planting young raspberries and cane fruits.

Pruning Start winter pruning on apples and pears to shape trees, thin out congested growth and remove damaged branches. On neglected, overgrown trees, remove complete branches to open up the head and let in more air and light.

Grape Vines Prune out fruited canes as soon as the leaves have fallen.

Fruit in store Check fruit regularly. Use the best fruits but remove any starting to show signs of softening or rot.

LAWN CARE

Mowing Cut grass if weather remains warm and dry setting the blades on a high cut, then trim the edges.

Repairs Mend any damaged edges and patch up worn areas of lawn.

Spiking Spike lawns with a hollow-tined aerator, and brush grit into the holes to create drainage channels. This is particularly useful on heavy, clay soils.

Top-dressing Spread a thin layer of gritty compost over the lawn surface to improve growth.

Care of mowers Service mowers before putting them into winter store. Sharpen the blades, clean well, then wipe all metal surfaces with an oily cloth. Empty out tanks on petrol mowers, and clean spark plugs. Store mowers in a dry and frost-free place, covered with an old sheet to keep them clean.

IN THE GREENHOUSE

Bulbs in pots When shoots are about 5cm (2in) tall, move potted bulbs from frames to a cool greenhouse to develop in full light, ready to bring indoors.

Hippeastrum Pot up large bulbs into 15-20cm (6-8in) pots. Soak the dry roots until they become plump, then plant bulbs to half their depth and place in a warm position to develop.

Watering Growing conditions are now much cooler and damper, so use water sparingly. Try not to wet plant leaves. The compost of many plants, like pelargoniums, can be allowed to dry out almost completely for the winter.

Cyclamen Keep in cool conditions and water sparingly from below. Feed every week with a liquid fertilizer.

Heating Check heaters daily, and use a max–min thermometer to ensure they are not set too high, wasting heat. Make sure the greenhouse is well insulated, but ventilate freely on warm days.

Propagators Small collections of tender plants and rooted cuttings can be over-wintered in a heated propagator. These are far cheaper to run than heating an entire greenhouse.

POND CARE

Plants Cut down marginal plants and remove dead leaves or flower stems from aquatic plants.

Netting Use a childs fishing net to remove leaves and other plant debris from the water.

Storing Remove pumps and filters and clean before storing away for winter.

Heating Float a pond heater in fish ponds to prevent ice forming. Electric heaters can be run on the supply used for pumps, now removed for winter.

LATE-AUTUMN CHECKLIST

❑ Collect ripe berries and fruits from trees and shrubs. Clean off their flesh in a sieve to reveal the seed and sow in pots. Place these in a cold frame to develop and raise new plants.

❑ Sweep up and collect leaves to keep the garden tidy and remove overwintering sites for slugs.

❑ Spread compost or manure over borders still to be dug. This will gradually be pulled down by worms. It also help insulate soil from frost so that it can still be dug during very cold weather.

❑ Wash cloches and cold frames inside and out.

❑ Clean and store flower pots and seed trays.

❑ Collect, clean and store canes and plant supports in a dry shed.

❑ Empty compost bins, sieving out well-rotted material to use while winter digging. Throw the remaining material back into the bin, mixing in a compost activator to kick start the process.

❑ Clean garden furniture and store under cover in shed.

❑ Move ceramic pots and any which are not frost-proof into the greenhouse for winter.

❑ Cover cold frames with old carpet or netting for extra insulation on cold nights.

❑ Order mail-order seed catalogues and place orders soon.

53

Cupressus arizonica var.
arizonica 'Blue Ice'

Early Winter – DECEMBER

*With the arrival of winter, day- and night- time temperatures drop,
so check that you have done all you can to protect tender plants
and any crops in store. The shorter days mean less hours to work
outside, but give more time for planning.*

THE FLOWER GARDEN

Roses Prune tall hybrid tea roses slightly to remove old flower stems and any dead or diseased wood.

Standard roses Reduce top growth to reduce damage from wind rock, but leave full pruning until early spring.

Perennials Finish cutting dead perennials down to soil level and tidy flower borders to remove plant debris that could harbour slugs, snails and other pests. Add it to the compost heap.

Wisteria Prune wisteria, shortening all side shoots back to about 2.5cm (1in), or two buds, from the main branch framework.

Borders Fork over bare patches between plants to relieve soil compaction, working garden compost into the soil as you go.

Mulching Spread straw or a bark mulch over the crowns of slightly tender plants, and round the base of tender climbers to provide extra protection from cold.

Planting Plant bare-rooted trees, shrubs and roses into well-prepared soil.

Propagating ivy Peg some low-growing ivy stems down to soil level to root and form new plants. Once well-rooted, detach from the parent plant and transplant elsewhere.

Holly If branches carrying berries will be needed as festive decorations, cover with nets as soon as possible to keep hungry birds away.

New features This is a good time to plan and construct new features, like rock gardens and ponds.

Shelter Build screens to protect newly planted conifers from cold winds.

Storing Regularly check bulbs, corms and tubers in store and remove any that show signs of rot. Ensure conditions are cool, dry and frost-free; dust with sulphur powder to prevent rotting diseases.

THE KITCHEN GARDEN

Digging Provided the soil is not frozen, carry out winter digging. Remove any old crops, clear weeds and dig in plenty of garden compost or rotted manure. Every third year dig a little deeper, forking the soil to a depth of at least 30–45cm (12–18in) to break up any compaction.

Soil testing Use a soil test kit or meter to check the acidity or alkalinity of your soil (the pH). Use this figure to determine whether the soil requires treating with lime to make it more alkaline or sulphur powder to make it more acid, aiming to produce a neutral soil preferred by most crops.

Vegetable crops

Onions Sow onion seed in pots or trays in the greenhouse for the biggest crops.

Asparagus Prepare beds for planting new asparagus in late winter or early spring. Order one-year-old crowns from a reliable mail-order supplier.

Brassicas Draw soil up round the stems of Brussels sprouts and other brassicas for support.

Protection Cover brassicas and other winter crops at risk from bird attack with netting or cloches. These can also provide extra protection for hardy peas, broad beans and other crops.

Celery Protect hardy trench celery with straw until ready to harvest.

Harvest Lift and store swede and

MONEY-SAVING TIPS
❖

- Re-use old flower pots and seed trays, scrubbing them clean inside and out, then soaking them in a solution of disinfectant.

- Clean, oil, sharpen and service your tools. Keep an oily rag handy to clean the blades and handles of tools before storing them for the winter. Spray metal surfaces with light oil to prevent them rusting.

- Install new water butts to the down pipes from the house, garage or greenhouse to save water from winter rains. If you pay for water on a meter this will save you money. Remember to empty and wash out existing water butts to remove accumulated dirt.

△ **THE SKILL OF RUNNING** *a productive kitchen garden is to plan for a continuity of crops for harvest right through the year. Choose varieties that mature at different times to extend the season.*

turnip for winter use.

Herbs Keep tender herbs cropping for longer by covering with cloches. Pot up a few roots of mint to grow an early crop either on the windowsill or in a cold frame.

Fruit crops

Fruit trees Plant fruit trees and bushes, choosing new, disease-resistant varieties where possible. Family fruit trees, where several varieties are grown as different branches on one tree, are a good choice for small gardens.

Rhubarb Place forcing jars over clumps of rhubarb and seakale to encourage early stems for picking.

Pruning Winter prune apple and pear trees to control their shape and vigour, removing weak, damaged, crossing or congested branches, and any showing signs of canker or disease.

Grape vines Prune outdoor grape vines.

IN THE GREENHOUSE

Perennials Check pelargoniums, fuchsias, argyranthemums and other overwintering plants, removing any dead or yellowing leaves.

Vines Prune greenhouse vines when all leaves have fallen and vine is dormant. Brush off loose bark that could be harbouring pests.

Chrysanthemums Cut down the tops of pot-grown late-flowering chrysanthemums to their base. Store in a greenhouse or cold frame.

Protection Bring potted peaches and nectarines under cover to reduce the spread of peach leaf curl disease.

Insulation Insulate greenhouses with bubble polythene or other materials.

Heating Check heaters daily to ensure they are working efficiently.

Cleaning Clean empty greenhouses, scrubbing down the frame and staging and cleaning the glass inside and out.

EARLY-WINTER CHECKLIST

❏ Scoop leaves and dead plant debris out of ponds.

❏ Tie string round upright-growing yew and conifers to prevent snow distorting their shape by pulling down branches.

❏ Write off for seed catalogues and place orders for potatoes, onion sets and shallots.

❏ Collect any remaining fallen autumn leaves, particularly if they are smothering alpines and border plants.

❏ Empty mature compost heaps and use the compost when winter digging.

❏ Treat timber posts, trellis and fencing with preservative now that many plants are dormant. Repair or replace loose or damaged fence panels.

❏ Thoroughly brush paths and steps to remove moss and slime.

❏ Make sure the water supply to outside taps has been turned off to prevent pipes bursting in the cold. Lag taps and pipework.

❏ Check tree stakes and ties and replace any that are loose, worn or damaged.

❏ Feed birds, especially in freezing weather, and put out fresh water each day. Hanging feeders close to fruit and roses encourages birds to forage on their stems for overwintering pests.

REMEMBER: *Avoid walking on frosted or waterlogged lawns.*

Mid-Winter – JANUARY

Long evenings indoors provide time to plan for the coming season and to place orders for plants and seed. There are still plenty of jobs to tempt you outside on bright days and, with the bare bones of the garden exposed, this is a good time to plan any major changes to the design and to move structures and plants around.

THE FLOWER GARDEN

Planting Continue planting trees, shrubs, hedging and roses.

Protection Use cloches to protect alpine plants outside from damage by winter cold and rain, or cover individual plants with a sheet of glass supported on wood or wire legs.

Bulbs Plant lilies in patio pots, keeping them in the greenhouse to develop.

Borders Be careful not to damage any emerging bulbs when forking over border soil.

TAKING ROOT CUTTINGS

Now is the time to take root cuttings from oriental poppies, acanthus, verbascum, Primula denticulata, Phlox paniculata, brunnera, anchusa, eryngium, gaillardia, romneya, rhus and many other plants. Either lift entire clumps or excavate soil from the edges to expose the roots. Cut off a few thick and healthy roots, using a straight cut. Most root cuttings are inserted vertically into pots of gritty compost; it is important that you keep this straight-cut end uppermost. Cut the sections of root about 2.5–5cm (1–2in) using a slanted cut, indicating that this end is inserted downwards. Several root sections can be put in a small pot, but the very fine roots of some perennials are best spread over the soil surface and covered with a thin layer of compost. Place in a frame or unheated greenhouse, and pot on individually once new shoots have started to develop.

THE KITCHEN GARDEN
Vegetable crops

Beans Enrich soil with compost where beans are to be grown.

Celery Prepare celery trenches, digging in plenty of garden compost.

Potatoes and onions Buy seed potatoes, shallots and onion sets. Sow onions in a heated propagator.

Warming up Cover soil needed for early sowings with cloches to warm it.

Rhubarb Place forcing jars over clumps of rhubarb and seakale.

Chicory Dig up chicory roots, pot up and cover to force chicons to develop.

Protection Bend large outer leaves over cauliflower curds to protect from cold and frost.

Storage Use fruit and vegetable crops in store; discard any showing signs of rot.

Fruit crops

Planting Plant fruit trees and bushes, choosing disease-resistant varieties where possible.

◁ **AFTER HEAVY SNOW FALL** *go round the garden with a broom and brush thick snow off evergreen shrubs and conifers, as the weight of snow can pull down or even break branches.*

MOVING SHRUBS

— ❖ —

Shrubs that have outgrown their allotted space, or which simply do not fit into the planting scheme, can be moved in this dormant season. Prepare the site to which the shrub will be moved, digging over the soil deeply and mixing in compost. To lift the shrub, use a spade to cut a circle of soil round it about 45–60cm (18–24in) from the stem. Excavate a trench of soil outside this circle, and start cutting inwards and under the shrub's roots to loosen it completely.

Ease a sheet of polythene or sacking under the rootball and tie firmly in place, then drag or lift the shrub to its new site. Replant, firming soil round the rootball, then water thoroughly. Before moving a very large shrub, prune out about a quarter of the oldest branches to reduce the plant's overall size and its subsequent demand for moisture.

57

IMPROVING YOUR SOIL

❖

- Dig over borders and vegetable plots or start cultivating new ground to prepare it for planting. Avoid digging soil which is waterlogged or frozen.

- Improve drainage on heavy, wet soils by mixing in generous quantities of gravel or sharp grit. All soils benefit from digging garden compost or well-rotted manure into the top layer.

- Cover areas still to be dug with a sheet of polythene to keep off rain and snow, ensuring that the soil remains dry enough for digging.

- On newly cultivated areas dig down to about twice the depth of your spade to break up the soil below. Thoroughly dig in compost at the rate of about one barrowload to the square metre.

DIGGING THE SOIL

❖

1 Divide your plot in half lengthwise and dig a trench the depth and width of your spade, running halfway across one end. Remove soil and pile it up outside the plot.

2 Spread a 5cm (2in) layer of organic matter in the bottom of the trench. Working backwards, dig along the edge of the trench, turning the soil over into it as you work. This fills the first trench with soil, creating a second trench alongside it.

3 Continue to dig and add organic matter, creating successive trenches. When you reach the end of the plot, work your way back up the other side. Fill in the last trench with soil removed from the first.

4 For double digging, make the trench the width of two spades. Dig organic matter into the base using a fork, breaking up the soil to the full depth of its prongs. Continue digging down the plot, turning the soil into successive double-width trenches. Use soil removed from the last trench to fill the first.

58

Pruning Prune old canes on autumn-fruiting raspberries down to soil level. Complete winter pruning of fruit trees, removing congested branches and pruning out damaged or diseased wood. Prune mature blackcurrant bushes, removing a quarter of the oldest branches at their base to encourage the production of healthy new growth.

Protection Make a polythene tent to prevent rain falling on wall-trained peaches and to reduce attack by peach leaf curl. Support the clear polythene on a framework of wooden battens, making sure you allow air in the sides and base for ventilation.

IN THE GREENHOUSE

Protecting Bring container-grown shrubs like camellias into a cold greenhouse for extra winter protection, and to encourage early flowering.

Sowing Sow seed of slow-maturing half-hardy summer bedding plants, like verbenas, pelargoniums and begonias, in heated propagators.

Cuttings Take cuttings from overwintered stools of greenhouse chrysanthemums, or order new plants.

Rhubarb Dig up crowns of rhubarb from the garden, place in pots in the greenhouse and cover to force early stems for picking.

Grape vines Prune greenhouse vines while completely dormant, and clean off dry bark from their rods in which pests can hide.

Pruning Winter prune climbers and shrubs like passiflora and bougainvillea.

Watering Water plants only sparingly during cool weather.

Cleaning Give greenhouses a thorough clean, scrubbing the framework and

MID-WINTER CHECKLIST

❏ Paint fences and trellis with timber preservative.

❏ Clean and tidy garden sheds.

❏ Wash and sterilize flower pots and seed trays, then stack ready to use.

❏ Inspect bulbs and tubers in store, removing any showing signs of rot.

❏ Sharpen blades on pruning tools.

❏ Send petrol mowers to be serviced.

❏ Buy in well rotted farmyard manure or mushroom compost to mulch borders and dig into soil.

❏ Bring potted bulbs into the home to flower.

❏ Clean grime and algae from patios and steps with a pressure washer, or scrub with a stiff broom.

❏ Take cuttings from conifers, rooting them in pots or trays.

❏ Order seeds and young plants from mail-order companies.

❏ Start keeping a gardening diary and record book and update it each week.

❏ Wrap sacking or bubble polythene round terracotta and ceramic containers to prevent them from freezing, or move them into a greenhouse.

❏ Lag garden taps and turn off the mains water supply to prevent pipes from freezing.

59

△ **BRING POTTED HYACINTH** *indoors to flower, keeping them in a cool, bright position. Turn pots daily to keep flowers growing upright, but stake blooms if they start to bend over.*

staging with disinfectant to remove dirt and overwintering pests. Use glass cleaner to remove dirt from glazing.
Heating Check that heaters are in good working order and fuel levels high enough to last the night. Remember to provide adequate ventilation if paraffin or gas heaters are being used.
Begonias Clean old compost off tubers kept in the pots since last summer. Replant in fresh compost. Keep warm.

COLD-WEATHER CHECKLIST

❖

• Firm soil which has been raised by frost back round plants.

• Knock snow from the branches of trees and shrubs to prevent damage.

• Avoid walking on lawns or pruning fruit trees if covered in frost.

• Do not let ice form on the surface of concrete pools as it can expand and damage the sides.

• Move tender plants or shrubs in containers to a sheltered site.

Late Winter – FEBRUARY

Although the cold weather, frosts and occasional snow make this a dormant season in the garden, some plants still brave the elements to put on a show. There are also plenty of tasks to complete and projects to develop before the arrival of warmer spring weather.

THE FLOWER GARDEN

Lilies Plump, healthy lily bulbs can be planted outside or in pots to provide flowers this summer.

Heathers Trim back winter-flowering heathers as soon as the flowers have started to fade. Trim varieties of *Erica carnea* with shears each year to keep growth compact, so plants do not become straggly and bare at the centre.

Snowdrops Lift and divide congested clumps of snowdrops after flowering, but while still in leaf or 'in the green'; new plants can also be purchased for planting now and these establish far better than planting dry bulbs.

PRUNING CLEMATIS
❖

Several large-flowered clematis hybrids may be pruned now by shortening long shoots down to a pair of swelling leaf buds. Some varieties and vigorous species can be pruned hard back to buds at the base of the main stem. All the previous season's growth of varieties like *C. tangutica* and *C. orientalis* can be pruned back to their woody stem framework or base. Although less vigorous, *C. texensis* can be pruned in a similar way, to buds at the base of stems. The non-twining *C. x durandii*, usually grown alongside a shrub for support, sends up new shoots from below soil level. Old dead stems can be removed completely.

Roses Plant new roses before spring. Bare-rooted bushes are still available for purchase by mail-order, and should be planted immediately on arrival, so prepare the site for them now.

Winter jasmine Prune after flowering, shortening long old shoots to encourage new growth from lower down the plant.

Ivy Clip wall-trained ivy, pulling it back from windows and gutters. Untidy, straggly and battered old foliage can be completely clipped back with shears; although plants look rather bare for a few months, fresh new leaves soon form.

Planting Continue planting new trees and shrubs, particularly bare-rooted subjects which must be planted while they are still dormant.

THE KITCHEN GARDEN

Digging Continue clearing ground, digging it over and adding garden compost. The surface can be left rough for the winter weather to break down and level, or it can be raked smooth.

Vegetable crops

Peas and beans Sow hardy peas and broad beans outside under cloches. Broad beans can also be sown in pots in the greenhouse for planting out later.

Seed sowing Sow early vegetable crops like carrots, spring onions and lettuce in cold frames or under cloches.

Potatoes Start chitting seed potatoes, standing them in trays in a light but frost-free position to encourage small shoots to form, ready to plant in spring.

Parsnips Sow as soon as soil conditions allow and complete before mid-spring.

Fruit crops

Pruning Finish winter pruning apple and pear trees, removing badly placed, damaged or diseased branches.

Strawberries Bring pot-grown plants into the greenhouse to encourage early flowering and fruiting.

Gooseberries Prune gooseberry bushes later this season, shortening side shoots and removing inward-growing branches to produce an open-centred bush which makes picking the fruits easier.

LATE-WINTER CHECKLIST

❏ Move patio containers to more sheltered sites during the worst weather to prevent frost damage.

❏ Keep sacking or old carpet handy to cover and insulate cold frames during very cold periods.

❏ Sprinkle sulphate of potash fertilizer round the base of fruit trees and bushes.

❏ If birds are damaging buds on fruit trees and bushes, cover with bird netting for protection.

❏ Clean and sharpen blades of pruners and garden tools. Then wipe with an oily cloth to protect from rust.

❏ Sweep paths and patios to remove any remaining autumn leaves.

❏ Wash the glass on cloches and cold frames both inside and out.

❏ Rake lawns to remove moss and thatch and to scatter worm casts that may have accumulated.

❏ Order a wide range of summer-flowering bulbs, corms and tubers for garden cultivation, including gladioli, dahlias, anemones, freesias, tigridia, ranunculus and acidanthera. Buy tuberous begonias and gloxinias for pots.

❏ Order seedlings and young bedding plants. These will be delivered later in spring to pot up and grow on to flowering size.

❏ Choose the best seed potatoes, shallots and onion sets from garden centres or order by post.

Peaches Spray with a copper-based fungicide to prevent peach leaf curl.
Figs Prune out the oldest branches from fan-trained figs on walls or fences. Tie in the new growth and pack straw back round stems to protect embryo fruits.

IN THE GREENHOUSE

Insulation Make sure greenhouses are well insulated with bubble polythene and draughts have been plugged. In heated greenhouses, insulation will dramatically reduce heating costs.
Sowing Continue sowing seed of summer bedding plants in heated propagators, including begonias, ageratum, pelargoniums, nicotiana, petunia, salvia and verbena. Most

△ SHADED WOODLAND FLOORS *become a carpet of colour from winter into spring. Leave bulbs to their own devices to set seed and spread.*

require a temperature of 18–21°C (65–70°F) for good germination.
Seedlings Prick out seedlings and space in larger trays as soon as they are large enough to handle by their new leaves. Never handle by their delicate stems which are easily crushed.
Bulbs Several bulbs, corms and tubers can be planted in pots now in a heated greenhouse, including dahlias, begonias, gloxinias and eucomis, among others.
Fuchsias Prune back the dead shoots on overwintered plants to their base to leave a well-shaped plant. New shoots will soon develop in a warm greenhouse.

ACKNOWLEDGMENTS

The producers and authors would like to thank the following for their support in the creation of this book: **Mrs P Mitchell**, **Mrs R Hills** and **Victoria Sanders** for allowing us to photograph in their gardens; **Paul Elding** and **Stuart Watson** at BOURNE VALLEY NURSERIES, Addlestone, Surrey for their advice, materials and studio.

PICTURE CREDITS

KEY: t = top; b = bottom; l = left; r = right; c = centre;
D = designer; G = garden

Neil Campbell-Sharp: G: Westwind 24r.

ELSOMS SEEDS LTD: 40r.

GARDEN FOLIO: **Graham Strong** 46r.

John Glover: 10t, 32r, 33br, 38b, 38t, 45r, 48l, 42l, 42r, 43br, 45r, 46bl, 46tr.

HARPUR GARDEN LIBRARY: D: Tessa King-Farlow 8r; Ron Simple 9b.

GARDEN AND WILDLIFE MATTERS PHOTO LIBRARY: 13bl, 16b, 22t, 23b, 31b, 58tr, 59, 60 all, 61tr; **David Cross** 17tl; **John Phipps** 15t, 16b; **Debi Wager** 17r.

Jacqui Hurst: G: Wreatham House 32bl.

Andrew Lawson: G: Barnsley House 6tr, 9t, 31t, 34t, 34b, 37b, 43bl, 45l, 48r, 53c, 54, 55, 59bl.

CLIVE NICHOLS GARDEN PICTURES: **Clive Nichols** G: Ivy Cottage, Dorset 4b; G: Heligan, Hampton Court Show 1998, 5tl; G: Bourton House, Glos 14b; G: Manoir Aux Quat Saisons, Oxon 20b; D: Rupert Golby, Chelsea 1995 29t; G: The Old Rectory, Berks 35b; D: Julie Toll 36r; G: National Asthma, Chelsea 1993 50; 53r; G: The Chef's Roof Garden, Chelsea 1999; D: Sir Terence Conran 56bl; **Graham Strong** 56tl, 57.

PHOTOS HORTICULTURAL PICTURE LIBRARY: 12t, 13t, 17t, 19b, 20t, 22b, 23t, 30b, 35t, 37t, 61bl.

DEREK ST ROMAINE PHOTOGRAPHY: **Derek St Romaine** G: Rosemoor 10l, 10r, 33bl, 38tl, 39r, 53tl, 54tl; D: Matthew Bell & Noula Hancock, Chelsea 1994 52bl, 53l, 54l.

THE GARDEN PICTURE LIBRARY: **David Askham** 28r; **Lynne Brotchie** 52br; **John Glover** 11tr, 32tl, 38tr, 46l, 46r; **Gil Hanly** 27l; **Michael Howes** 28l; **Jacqui Hurst** 21t 32b; **Mayer/Le Scanff** 6l, 26l, 26r, 44bl; **Howard Rice** 29b, 47bl; **Friedrich Strauss** 44br; **Juliette Wade** 6t.

AL TOZER LTD: 40l.

ADDITIONAL PHOTOGRAPHY: **Peter Anderson** 3br, 6b, 11bl, 11bc, 11br, 19l, 19m, 19tr, 21b, 25br, 33t, 39l, 41b, 43t, 49tl, 49r. **Steve Gorton**, 1, 3tr, 5br, 18 all, 25tl, 25bl, 25bc, 27 all, 32tl, 44tr, 47tr, 49bl, 51t, 52t.

A-Z BOTANICAL **Shelia Orme** G: Dry Stanford Manor, Oxon 51b; **Geoff Kidd** 54b.

Maurice Walker 58bl.